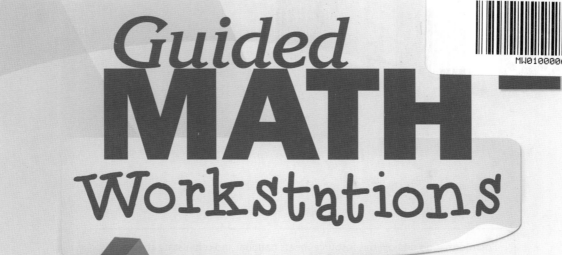

Guided MATH Workstations

Anika ate $\frac{1}{4}$ of her sandwich.
Show $\frac{1}{4}$ on each model.

Authors

Donna Boucher

Laney Sammons, M.L.S.

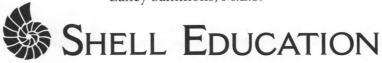

SHELL EDUCATION

For information on how this resource meets national and other state standards, see pages 13–14. You may also review this information by visiting our website at www.teachercreatedmaterials.com/administrators/correlations/ and following the on-screen directions.

Publishing Credits

Corinne Burton, M.A.Ed., *President*; Conni Medina, M.A.Ed., *Managing Editor*; Diana Kenney M.A.Ed., NBCT, *Content Director*; Veronique Bos, *Creative Director*; Robin Erickson, *Art Director*; Kristy Stark, M.A.Ed., *Editor*; Fabiola Sepulveda, *Graphic Designer*; Kyleena Harper, *Assistant Editor*

Image Credits

All images from iStock and Shutterstock.

Standards

Shell Education

A division of Teacher Created Materials
5301 Oceanus Drive
Huntington Beach, CA 92649-1030

http://www.tcmpub.com/shell-education

ISBN 978-1-4258-1729-9
©2018 Shell Educational Publishing, Inc.

Table of Contents

Introduction

GUIDE Workstation Tasks

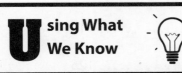

Table of Contents *(cont.)*

Independent Math Work

Developing Fluency

Expressing Mathematical Ideas

Appendices

The Guided Math Framework

Guided Math (Sammons 2010, 2014) is an instructional framework that helps teachers provide quality mathematics instruction for their students. Teachers address their students' varied learning needs within a carefully planned numeracy-rich environment where students are challenged to not just *do* math but instead *become* mathematicians. Implemented together, Guided Math's seven components are designed to help students as they develop a deep conceptual understanding of math, acquire computational fluency, and become skilled in thinking and acting mathematically.

Figure I.1 Instructional Components of Guided Math

Classroom Environment of Numeracy (Daily)
Students are immersed in a classroom environment that contains evidence of real-life math tasks, data analysis, math word walls, measuring tools, mathematical communication, class-created math anchor charts, graphic organizers, calendars, and authentic problem-solving challenges.
Math Warm-Ups (Daily)
This daily appetizer prepares students for "Your Choice" entrees with Math Stretches, calendar activities, problems of the day, reviews of skills to be maintained, and previews of skills to come.
Whole-Class Instruction (Your Choice)
Students are instructed as a whole group to activate prior knowledge, to model and think aloud, to read math-related literature aloud, to review and assess, or for Math Huddles.
Small-Group Instruction (Your Choice)
Students are instructed in small groups based on student needs to introduce new concepts, practice new skills, work with manipulatives, provide intensive and targeted instruction to struggling learners, provide additional challenge, introduce Math Workshop activities, and conduct informal assessments.
Math Workshop (Your Choice)
Students work independently, either individually, in pairs, or in groups, on tasks that may include extensions of other activities, mastered skills, investigations, math games, math journals, or interdisciplinary work, while teachers conduct small-group lessons and conferences.
Conferences (Daily)
Teachers confer with students to assess understanding, provide opportunities for math communication, determine instructional needs, and deliver brief teaching points.
Assessment (Daily)
Students are assessed through observation, on final work products, and during mathematical conversations. Assessment *for* learning and *of* learning are key to informing instruction.

(Sammons 2010)

What Is Math Workshop?

Math Workshop is a key ingredient of success in a Guided Math classroom (Sammons 2010, 2013). As one of the most versatile components of the framework, it accommodates a vast array of learning tasks. Not only does it provide opportunities for students to learn how to work independently on worthwhile mathematical endeavors, it also allows teachers to work with small groups or to confer with individual students.

During Math Workshop, students work independently—individually, in pairs, or in groups—and participate in Math Workstation tasks that have been designed to provide ongoing practice of previously mastered concepts and skills, to promote computational fluency, and to encourage mathematical curiosity and inquiry. In the first weeks of school, students learn and repeatedly practice the routines and procedures that make Math Workshop function smoothly. As students assume greater independence for their learning during Math Workshop, teachers may then expand their teaching roles.

Figure I.2 The Roles of Teachers and Students during Math Workshop

Teachers	Students
• Teach small-group lessons • Conduct math conferences • Informally assess learning through observations • Facilitate mathematical learning and curiosity through questioning	• Assume responsibility for their learning and behavior • Function as fledgling mathematicians • Communicate mathematically with peers • Review and practice previously mastered concepts and skills • Improve computational fluency • Increase ability to work cooperatively with peers

What Are Math Workstations?

Workstations are collections of tasks stored together and worked on independently of the teacher by students in specified workspaces. Students often work in pairs or small groups but may work alone. Each station contains a variety of carefully selected math tasks to support mathematical learning. Some of the tasks may be mandatory, while others may be optional. Essential for an effective Math Workshop is the inclusion of high-quality, appropriate tasks in the workstations. By grappling with these tasks independently, students gain greater mathematical proficiency and confidence in their mathematical abilities. Here, students "practice problem solving while reasoning, representing, communicating, and making connections among mathematical topics as the teacher observes and interacts with individuals at work or meets with a small group for differentiated math instruction" (Diller 2011, 7).

Math Centers versus Math Workstations

For many years, classrooms contained Math Centers where learners worked independently. Math Centers were considerably different from today's Math Workstations. Even the label *Math Workstation* clearly sends the message that students are expected to work as mathematicians. Workstation tasks are not included for fun alone but to further students' understanding of math, improve their computational fluency, and increase their mathematical competency. The chart below highlights the differences between Math Centers and Math Workstations.

Figure I.3 Math Centers Versus Math Workstations

Math Centers	Math Workstations
• Games and activities are introduced to students when distributed at centers and are rarely used for instructional purposes.	• Tasks are derived from materials previously used during instruction, so students are already familiar with them.
• Centers are often thematic and change weekly.	• Tasks are changed for instructional purposes, not because it is the end of the week.
• Centers are often made available to students after they complete their regular work.	• Tasks provide ongoing practice to help students retain and deepen their understanding and are an important part of students' mathematical instruction.
• All students work on the same centers, and activities are seldom differentiated.	• Tasks are differentiated to meet the identified learning needs of students.

The GUIDE Model

The GUIDE model provides a simple and efficient organizational system for Math Workshop. With this model there are five Math Workstations, each with a menu of tasks from which students may work. The workstation tasks may be required, optional, or a combination of the two. You as the teacher decide which best meets the needs of your students. Instead of rotating from station to station, students work on only one station per day. By the end of a week, however, students will have worked at all five GUIDE stations.

The GUIDE acronym stands for the following:

Games for Mathematicians: Math games used to maintain previously mastered mathematical concepts and skills and promote computational proficiency

Using What We Know: Problem solving or challenge activities to draw upon mathematical understanding and skills

Independent Math Work: Materials used to teach previously mastered content incorporated into workstation tasks (paper-and-pencil tasks may be included)

Developing Fluency: Tasks that help students develop number sense and mental math skills

Expressing Mathematical Ideas: Tasks with opportunities to solidify mathematical vocabulary and encourage communication (math journals or math vocabulary notebooks may be included)

Students may be given the choice of where they will work each day, or the teacher may make team assignments. If you allow your students to choose their stations, provide a weekly checklist to track completed stations. Using the checklist, they will clearly see which stations they still need to complete by the end of the week.

This model offers maximum flexibility to teachers. Not only can the composition of small-group lessons be changed at a moment's notice to respond to newly identified student needs, but the length of the lessons may also vary from group to group. Teachers also appreciate another aspect of the flexibility this model offers. If the Math Workshop schedule is interrupted for some reason (e.g., testing day, holiday, whole-group lesson), the rotation schedule simply continues the next day as Math Workshop resumes. So, if a student does *G* on Monday, *U* on Tuesday, and then there is no workshop on Wednesday, he or she would do *I* on Thursday. As a result, students might not do all five workstations in one week, but they would still get to do them all after five Math Workshop days.

Differentiating Math Workstation Tasks

It is important that workstation tasks are differentiated to meet the unique needs of learners. Task Menus should clearly indicate which tasks have these options, and directions for these tasks should explain each of the options. Students need to know not only what the options are, but also which of them they should complete. Rather than labeling the options by ability level, various options for differentiation may be indicated by color, shape, or other symbol. For example, if there are three options, one might be coded with a circle, one with a triangle, and one with a square. Let students know which options they will complete by assigning them to the shape that best meets their learning needs.

While much focus has been placed on differentiation for struggling students, differentiation for those who may need extra challenge is equally important. There are several ways to provide differentiation. Tasks may be differentiated by:

- **Providing completely different tasks**—In some instances, students at one workstation will work on completely different tasks to address identified needs.

- **Providing variations of the same task**—This is the most efficient way to differentiate Math Workstation tasks because students work on the same task with some variations, so it can be introduced to everyone at the same time rather than having to introduce different tasks for different students. The task might be differentiated by changing the numbers, operations involved, or other aspects of the task to make it appropriate for all learners. Students who struggle with reading may require a recording of the task directions or other written materials. Some students may need to have manipulatives available. Others may benefit from having vocabulary cards with visual representations as references. Consider students' needs and offer support, if necessary, but use your professional judgment to avoid providing ongoing supports that become crutches rather than scaffolds for learning. Each task provided in this resource offers suggestions for differentiation to address individual students' needs.

- **Providing multiple ways for students to show their learning**—Students who struggle may benefit from the use of manipulatives to demonstrate their mathematical understanding. Students who need a challenge may create graphic organizers to display their work or graphs to represent data.

How to Use This Book

The tasks in this book have been designed for use with the GUIDE Workshop Model, but they may be incorporated into any workshop model you choose. It is important to model and practice these workstation tasks and the sentence stems on the *Talking Points* cards with students before expecting students to complete them independently.

Workstation Organization

An **overview** of the lesson, materials, objective, procedure, and differentiation is provided for the teacher on the first page of each GUIDE workstation task.

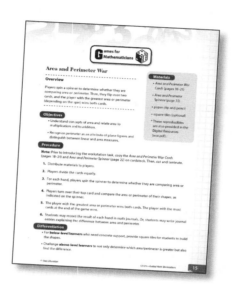

A **Student Task card** with directions and a materials list is provided for easy implementation and organization. Students may use the materials list as they put away their math workstation task so that all materials are included.

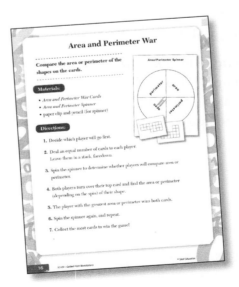

A **Talking Points card** with math vocabulary words and sentence stems is provided to encourage mathematical discourse. Consider copying it on brightly colored paper to draw students' attention. Laminate and store it with the student task card and other resources for each workstation task.

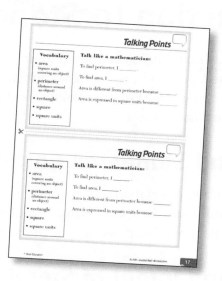

Additional **resources** for each task (e.g., spinners, cards, activity sheets) are included.

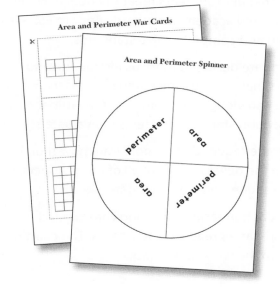

Digital resources to support the workstation tasks in this book are available online. A complete list of available documents is provided on pages 140. To access the digital resources, go to this website: **http://www.tcmpub.com/download-files**. Enter this code: 63068562. Follow the on-screen directions.

Introduction to Standards Correlations

Shell Educational Publishing is committed to producing educational materials that are research- and standards-based. In this effort, we have correlated all of our products to the academic standards of all 50 states, the District of Columbia, the Department of Defense Dependents Schools, and all Canadian provinces.

How to Find Standards Correlations

To print a customized correlation report of this product for your state, visit our website at **http://www.tcmpub.com/shell-education**. If you require assistance in printing correlation reports, please contact our Customer Service Department at 1-877-777-3450.

Purpose and Intent of Standards

The Every Student Succeeds Act (ESSA) mandates that all states adopt challenging academic standards that help students meet the goal of college and career readiness. While many states already adopted academic standards prior to ESSA, the act continues to hold states accountable for detailed and comprehensive standards.

Standards are designed to focus instruction and guide adoption of curricula. Standards are statements that describe the criteria necessary for students to meet specific academic goals. They define the knowledge, skills, and content students should acquire at each level. Standards are also used to develop standardized tests to evaluate students' academic progress.

Teachers are required to demonstrate how their lessons meet state standards. State standards are used in the development of all of our products, so educators can be assured they meet the academic requirements of each state.

The workstation tasks in this book are aligned to today's national and state-specific college-and-career readiness standards. The chart on pages 13–14 shows the correlation of those standards to the workstation tasks.

Standards Correlations

Workstation Task	College-and-Career Readiness Standard(s)
Area and Perimeter War (page 15)	Understand concepts of area and relate area to multiplication and to addition. Recognize perimeter as an attribute of plane figures and distinguish between linear and area measures.
Difference from 5,000 (page 23)	Use place value understanding and properties of operations to multiply two 2-digit numbers.
On a Roll (page 29)	Build fractions from unit fractions by applying and extending previous understandings of operations of whole numbers. Add and subtract fractions referring to the same whole and having like denominators.
Equivalent Fractions (page 33)	Recognize and generate equivalent fractions.
Exploring Manipulatives (page 39)	Explore with math manipulatives. Describe observations using words and pictures.
$1,000 House (page 42)	Generalize place value understanding for multi-digit whole numbers.
Choose Sides (page 46)	Construct viable arguments. Critique the reasoning of others.
I Wonder… (page 55)	Make sense of problems. Reason about quantities.
You Write the Story (page 62)	Represent and solve one and two-step problems involving all four operations.
Follow the Rule (page 68)	Generate additive and multiplicative number patterns using an input-output table and given rule.

Lining Up Equivalent Fractions (page 77)	Demonstrate understanding that a fraction can be shown as a number on a number line and two fractions are equivalent if they are located at the same point on a number line.
Measurement Conversion (page 85)	Convert like measurement units within a given measurement system.
Numberless Word Problems (page 90)	Solve problems with whole numbers using the four operations. Represent problems using equations with a letter standing for the unknown quantity.
Multiples Tic-Tac-Toe (page 97)	Determine whether a given whole number is a multiple of a given one-digit number.
Multiplication Move One (page 109)	Multiply factors to build automaticity with math facts.
Twenty-One (page 114)	Use whole number operations to interpret numerical expressions.
Par for the Course (page 119)	Add, subtract, and multiply to build automaticity with math facts.
This Reminds Me Of… (page 125)	Recognize connections between mathematical concepts. Use precise language to communicate relationships.
Wanted Vocabulary Poster (page 131)	Use precise language to communicate mathematical ideas. Make connections between related mathematical concepts.
All About… (page 136)	Use precise mathematical language, numbers, and/or drawings to represent a mathematical concept.

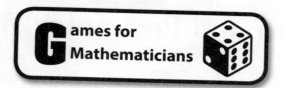

G ames for **Mathematicians**

Area and Perimeter War

Overview

Players spin a spinner to determine whether they are comparing area or perimeter. Then, they flip over two cards, and the player with the greatest area or perimeter (depending on the spin) wins both cards.

Objectives

- Understand concepts of area and relate area to multiplication and to addition.

- Recognize perimeter as an attribute of plane figures and distinguish between linear and area measures.

Procedure

Note: Prior to introducing the workstation task, copy the *Area and Perimeter War Cards* (pages 18–21) and *Area and Perimeter Spinner* (page 22) on cardstock. Then, cut and laminate.

1. Distribute materials to players.

2. Players divide the cards equally.

3. For each hand, players spin the spinner to determine whether they are comparing area or perimeter.

4. Players turn over their top card and compare the area or perimeter of their shapes, as indicated on the spinner.

5. The player with the greatest area or perimeter wins the cards. The player with the most cards at the end of the game wins.

6. Students may record the result of each hand in math journals or write journal entries explaining the difference between area and perimeter.

Differentiation

- For **below-level learners** who need concrete support, provide square tiles for students to build the shapes.

- Challenge **above-level learners** to not only determine which area/perimeter is greater but also find the difference.

Materials

- *Area and Perimeter War Cards* (pages 18–21)

- *Area and Perimeter Spinner* (page 22)

- paper clip and pencil

- square tiles (optional)

* The *Talking Points* card and these reproducibles are also provided in the Digital Resources (war.pdf).

Area and Perimeter War

Collect the most cards by comparing the area or perimeter of the shapes on the cards.

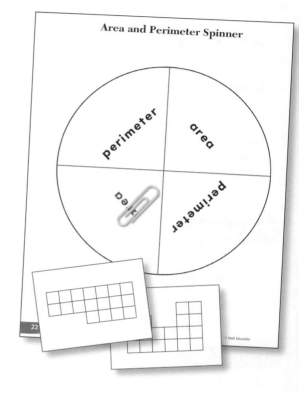

Materials

- *Area and Perimeter War Cards*
- *Area and Perimeter Spinner*
- paper clip and pencil (for spinner)

Directions

1. Decide which player will go first.

2. Deal an equal number of cards to each player. Leave them in a stack, facedown.

3. Spin the spinner to determine whether players will compare area or perimeter.

4. Both players turn over their top card and find the area or perimeter (depending on the spin) of their shape.

5. The player with the greatest area or perimeter wins the cards.

6. Spin the spinner again and repeat.

7. Collect the most cards to win the game!

Talking Points

Vocabulary
• **area** (square units covering an object)
• **perimeter** (distance around an object)
• **rectangle**
• **square**
• **square units**

Talk like a mathematician:

To find perimeter, I _____ .

To find area, I _____ .

Area is different from perimeter because _____ .

Area is expressed in square units because _____ .

✄ -

Talking Points

Vocabulary
• **area** (square units covering an object)
• **perimeter** (distance around an object)
• **rectangle**
• **square**
• **square units**

Talk like a mathematician:

To find perimeter, I _____ .

To find area, I _____ .

Area is different from perimeter because _____ .

Area is expressed in square units because _____ .

Area and Perimeter War Cards

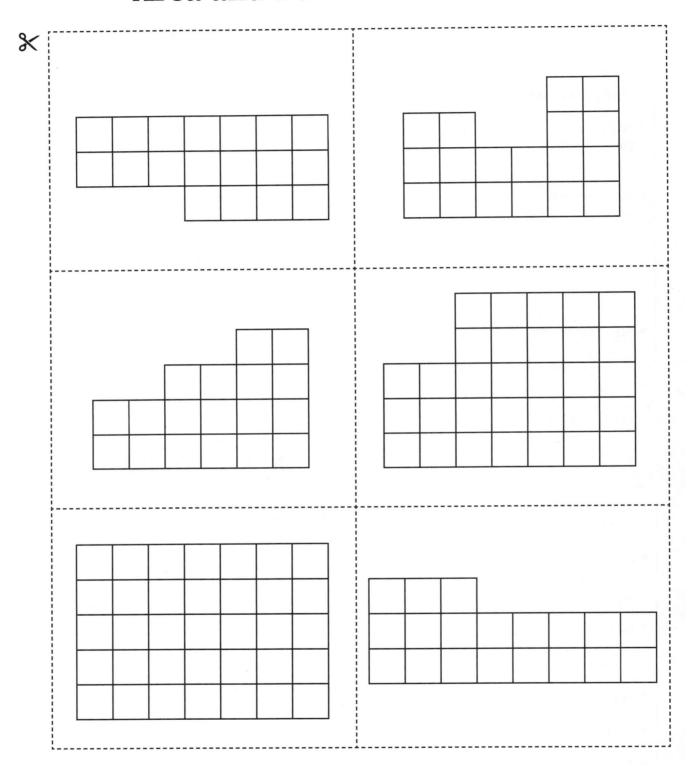

51729—Guided Math Workstations

Area and Perimeter War Cards *(cont.)*

Area and Perimeter War Cards *(cont.)*

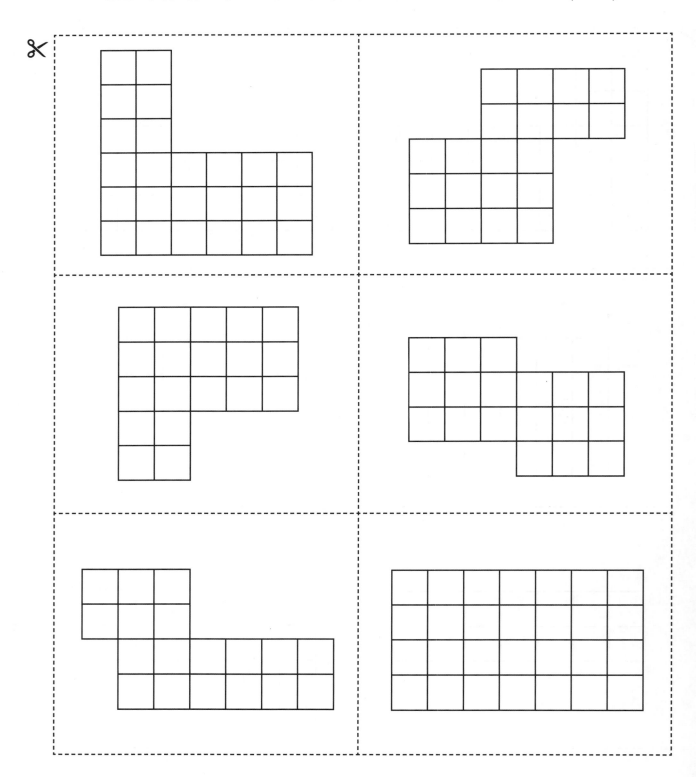

Area and Perimeter War Cards *(cont.)*

Area and Perimeter Spinner

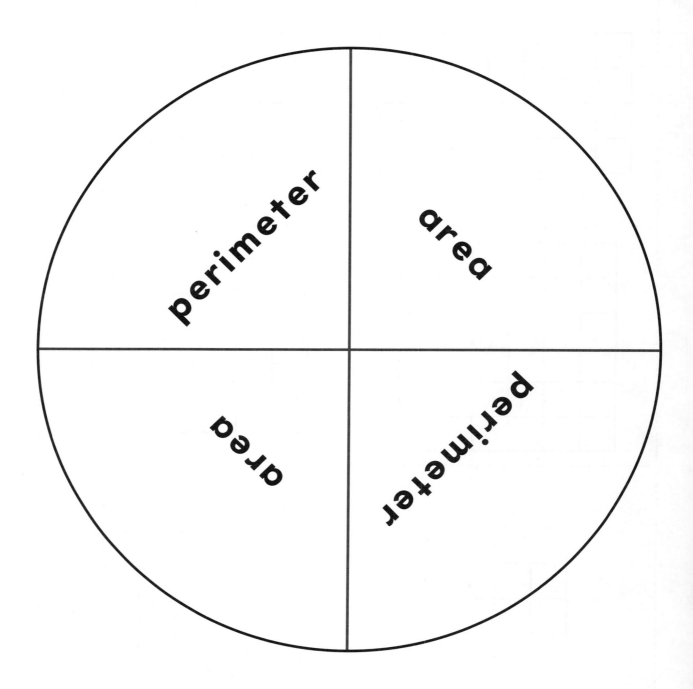

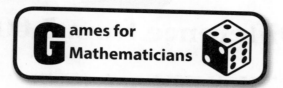

Difference from 5,000

Overview

Students roll a number cube to create two 2-digit factors and use an area model to find the product. After four rounds, students add their products and find the difference from 5,000. The player with the smallest difference wins.

Materials

- 1 number cube per player

- *Difference from 5,000* recording sheet (pages 26–27)

- *Multiplication Chart* (optional) (page 28)

* The *Talking Points* card and these reproducibles are also provided in the Digital Resources (difference.pdf).

Objective

Use place value understanding and properties of operations to multiply two 2-digit numbers.

Procedure

1. Distribute two-sided copies of the *Difference from 5,000* recording sheet (pages 26–27) and other materials to students.

2. Players roll the number cube four times, record the digits, and use the four digits to create a 2-digit by 2-digit multiplication problem. They may use the digits in any combination. For example, a roll of 2, 5, 3, and 6 could create any of the following possible multiplication problems: 25 × 36, 35 × 26, or 32 × 56.

3. Players use an area model to find the product.

4. After four rounds, players add their four products and determine the difference from 5,000.

5. The player with the smallest difference wins the game.

6. Students may show their thinking on copies of their recording sheets or write journal entries explaining strategies used.

Differentiation

- Provide a *Multiplication Chart* (page 28) to **below-level learners** who are not fluent with their multiplication facts. Students can roll the number cube three times to create a 1-digit by 2-digit multiplication problem, rather than 2-digit by 2-digit.

- Challenge **above-level learners** to determine all of the different 2-digit by 2-digit combinations they can create with the four digits they roll.

Difference from 5,000

Have the smallest difference from 5,000 after four rounds of creating and multiplying 2-digit numbers.

×	**tens**	**ones**
ones		
tens		

Materials

- 1 number cube for each player
- *Difference from 5,000* recording sheet
- *Multiplication Chart* (optional)

Directions

1. Take turns:

   - Roll a number cube four times. Record the digits on the *Difference from 5,000* recording sheet.
   - Put the numbers in any order to create a 2-digit by 2-digit multiplication problem. For example, a roll of 2, 5, 3, and 6 could create any of the following possible multiplication problems: 25 × 36, 35 × 26, or 32 × 56.
   - Estimate the product.
   - Multiply the factors using an area model.

2. After four rounds, add all four products and calculate the difference of your sum from 5,000.

3. The player with the smallest difference wins.

Talking Points

Vocabulary

- digit
- partial product
- sum
- difference
- area model

$4 \times 8 = 32$
factors product

Talk like a mathematician:

My factors are _____ and _____.

The product of _____ and _____ is _____.

The strategy I used to form my 2-digit numbers is _____.

I can find the difference from 5,000 by _____.

_____ has the smallest difference because _____.

It helps to estimate because _____.

✂ -

Talking Points

Vocabulary

- digit
- partial product
- sum
- difference
- area model

$4 \times 8 = 32$
factors product

Talk like a mathematician:

My factors are _____ and _____.

The product of _____ and _____ is _____.

The strategy I used to form my 2-digit number is _____.

I can find the difference from 5,000 by _____.

_____ has the smallest difference because _____.

It helps to estimate because _____.

Difference from 5,000

Digits: _____, _____, _____, and _____

Multiplication problem: _____

Estimate: _____

×	tens	ones
ones		
tens		

Digits: _____, _____, _____, and _____

Multiplication problem: _____

Estimate: _____

×	tens	ones
ones		
tens		

Digits: _____, _____, _____, and _____

Multiplication problem: _____

Estimate: _____

×	**tens**	**ones**
ones		
tens		

Digits: _____, _____, _____, and _____

Multiplication problem: _____

Estimate: _____

×	**tens**	**ones**
ones		
tens		

Add your four products.

Calculate the difference of the sum of your products from 5,000.

Multiplication Chart

	1	2	3	4	5	6	7	8	9	10	11	12
1	1	2	3	4	5	6	7	8	9	10	11	12
2	2	4	6	8	10	12	14	16	18	20	22	24
3	3	6	9	12	15	18	21	24	27	30	33	36
4	4	8	12	16	20	24	28	32	36	40	44	48
5	5	10	15	20	25	30	35	40	45	50	55	60
6	6	12	18	24	30	36	42	48	54	60	66	72
7	7	14	21	28	35	42	49	56	63	70	77	84
8	8	16	24	32	40	48	56	64	72	80	88	96
9	9	18	27	36	45	54	63	72	81	90	99	108
10	10	20	30	40	50	60	70	80	90	100	110	120
11	11	22	33	44	55	66	77	88	99	110	121	132
12	12	24	36	48	60	72	84	96	108	120	132	144

 51729—Guided Math Workstations

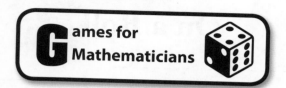

Games for **Mathematicians**

On a Roll

Overview

Students roll number cubes to create six fractions with like denominators, add the fractions, and convert the improper fractions to mixed numbers.

Objectives

- Build fractions from unit fractions by applying and extending previous understandings of operations of whole numbers.
- Add and subtract fractions referring to the same whole and having like denominators.

Procedure

1. Distribute copies of the *On a Roll* recording sheet (page 32) and other materials to students.

2. Player 1 rolls the number cube. All players use that number as the denominator for their fractions.

3. Players take turns rolling the number cube six more times to determine the numerators.

4. Players add their six fractions to create improper fractions. Then, they convert the improper fractions to mixed numbers.

5. Players check each other's work. The player with the largest sum earns a point.

6. Repeat four times.

7. Students may record their thinking on their recording sheets or create posters to show and explain the equivalency between one pair of their improper fractions and mixed numbers.

Differentiation

- You may choose to provide **below-level learners** with fraction tiles to use as a concrete model, or print and cut *Fraction Tiles* (fractiontiles.pdf) from the Digital Resources.
- Have **above-level learners** use a different denominator for their fractions than their opponents, making it more of a challenge to compare the sums.

On a Roll

Earn points by creating the largest improper fraction or mixed number.

Materials

- *On a Roll* recording sheet
- 1 number cube for each player

Directions

1. Player 1:

   - Roll the number cube.
   - All players use the number rolled as the denominator.

2. Take turns:

   - Roll 6 more times to complete the numerators.
   - Add the fractions to create an improper fraction.
   - Convert the improper fraction to a mixed number.

3. The player with the greatest sum gets 1 point.

4. Continue for 4 more rounds.

5. The player with the most points wins.

Talking Points

Vocabulary

- addend
- sum
- greater than
- less than

$\dfrac{3}{4}$ ← numerator
← denominator

$\dfrac{5}{2}$ ← improper fraction

$1\dfrac{2}{3}$ ← mixed number

Talk like a mathematician:

A denominator of _____ means _____ equal parts.

This is an improper fraction because _____.

A mixed number can be expressed as an equivalent improper fraction by _____.

One strategy I can use to convert an improper fraction to a mixed number is _____.

✂ -

Talking Points

Vocabulary

- addend
- sum
- greater than
- less than

$\dfrac{3}{4}$ ← numerator
← denominator

$\dfrac{5}{2}$ ← improper fraction

$1\dfrac{2}{3}$ ← mixed number

Talk like a mathematician:

A denominator of _____ means _____ equal parts.

This is an improper fraction because _____.

A mixed number can be expressed as an equivalent improper fraction by _____.

One strategy I can use to convert an improper fraction to a mixed number is _____.

Name: _____ Date: _____

On a Roll

		Improper fraction	Mixed number

___ + ___ + ___ + ___ + ___ + ___ = ___ ___

		Improper fraction	Mixed number

___ + ___ + ___ + ___ + ___ + ___ = ___ ___

		Improper fraction	Mixed number

___ + ___ + ___ + ___ + ___ + ___ = ___ ___

		Improper fraction	Mixed number

___ + ___ + ___ + ___ + ___ + ___ = ___ ___

		Improper fraction	Mixed number

___ + ___ + ___ + ___ + ___ + ___ = ___ ___

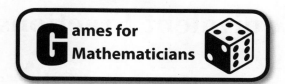

Games for **Mathematicians**

Equivalent Fractions

Overview

Students try to capture four spaces in a row by creating equivalent fractions.

Objective

Recognize and generate equivalent fractions.

Procedure

Note: Prior to the lesson, copy the *Equivalent Fractions Game Board* (page 36) and the *Equivalent Fractions Cards* (page 37) on cardstock, and cut and laminate.

1. Players shuffle the cards and place them facedown in a draw pile.

2. Players take turns. Each player will:

   • draw a card;

   • find a fraction on the game board equivalent to the fraction on the card;

   • justify the equivalence; and

   • cover or mark that space.

3. The first player to mark four spaces in a row (horizontally, vertically, or diagonally) is the winner.

4. Students may document their equivalent fraction pairs in their math journals.

Differentiation

• You may choose to provide **below-level learners** with copies of the *Multiplication Chart* (page 38) to help them. For example, the rows marked 1 and 3 show fractions equivalent to $\frac{1}{3}$, $\frac{2}{6}$, $\frac{3}{9}$, and so on.

• Challenge **above-level learners** to choose pairs of cards and either add or subtract the fractions.

Materials

• *Equivalent Fractions Game Board* (page 36)

• *Equivalent Fractions Cards* (page 37)

• counters (two colors)

• *Multiplication Chart* (page 38) (optional)

* The *Talking Points* card and these reproducibles are also provided in the Digital Resources (equivalent.pdf).

Equivalent Fractions

Capture four spaces in a row by creating equivalent fractions.

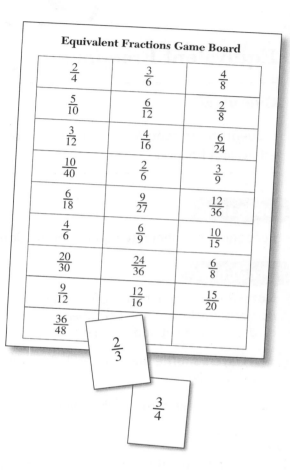

Equivalent Fractions Game Board

$\frac{2}{4}$	$\frac{3}{6}$	$\frac{4}{8}$
$\frac{5}{10}$	$\frac{6}{12}$	$\frac{2}{8}$
$\frac{3}{12}$	$\frac{4}{16}$	$\frac{6}{24}$
$\frac{10}{40}$	$\frac{2}{6}$	$\frac{3}{9}$
$\frac{6}{18}$	$\frac{9}{27}$	$\frac{12}{36}$
$\frac{4}{6}$	$\frac{6}{9}$	$\frac{10}{15}$
$\frac{20}{30}$	$\frac{24}{36}$	$\frac{6}{8}$
$\frac{9}{12}$	$\frac{12}{16}$	$\frac{15}{20}$
$\frac{36}{48}$		

$\frac{2}{3}$

$\frac{3}{4}$

Materials

- *Equivalent Fractions Cards*
- *Equivalent Fractions Game Board*
- counters (two colors)
- *Multiplication Chart* (optional)

Directions

1. Shuffle the *Equivalent Fractions Cards*. Place them facedown in a pile.

2. Take turns doing the following:

   - Draw a card from the pile.
   - Find a fraction on the board equivalent to the fraction on your card.
   - Justify your thinking about why the fractions are equivalent.
   - Cover or mark a space that contains the equivalent fraction.

3. The first player to mark four spaces in a row (horizontally, vertically, or diagonally) is the winner.

 51729—Guided Math Workstations

Talking Points

Vocabulary

- equivalent fraction
- numerator
- denominator

Talk like a mathematician:

To make an equivalent fraction, I _____.

I know _____ and _____ are equivalent because _____.

A pattern I notice is _____.

✂ -

Talking Points

Vocabulary

- equivalent fraction
- numerator
- denominator

Talk like a mathematician:

To make an equivalent fraction, I _____.

I know _____ and _____ are equivalent because _____.

A pattern I notice is _____.

Equivalent Fractions Game Board

$\frac{1}{4}$	$\frac{3}{4}$	$\frac{1}{3}$	$\frac{1}{4}$	$\frac{1}{3}$
$\frac{1}{2}$	$\frac{1}{3}$	$\frac{3}{4}$	$\frac{2}{3}$	$\frac{1}{4}$
$\frac{2}{3}$	$\frac{3}{4}$	$\frac{1}{4}$	$\frac{3}{4}$	$\frac{1}{2}$
$\frac{1}{3}$	$\frac{2}{3}$	$\frac{1}{2}$	$\frac{1}{4}$	$\frac{2}{3}$
$\frac{1}{2}$	$\frac{3}{4}$	$\frac{2}{3}$	$\frac{1}{3}$	$\frac{1}{2}$

Equivalent Fractions Cards

$\frac{2}{4}$	$\frac{3}{6}$	$\frac{4}{8}$
$\frac{5}{10}$	$\frac{6}{12}$	$\frac{2}{8}$
$\frac{3}{12}$	$\frac{4}{16}$	$\frac{6}{24}$
$\frac{10}{40}$	$\frac{2}{6}$	$\frac{3}{9}$
$\frac{6}{18}$	$\frac{9}{27}$	$\frac{12}{36}$
$\frac{4}{6}$	$\frac{6}{9}$	$\frac{10}{15}$
$\frac{20}{30}$	$\frac{24}{36}$	$\frac{6}{8}$
$\frac{9}{12}$	$\frac{12}{16}$	$\frac{15}{20}$
$\frac{36}{48}$		

Multiplication Chart

	1	2	3	4	5	6	7	8	9	10	11	12
1	1	2	3	4	5	6	7	8	9	10	11	12
2	2	4	6	8	10	12	14	16	18	20	22	24
3	3	6	9	12	15	18	21	24	27	30	33	36
4	4	8	12	16	20	24	28	32	36	40	44	48
5	5	10	15	20	25	30	35	40	45	50	55	60
6	6	12	18	24	30	36	42	48	54	60	66	72
7	7	14	21	28	35	42	49	56	63	70	77	84
8	8	16	24	32	40	48	56	64	72	80	88	96
9	9	18	27	36	45	54	63	72	81	90	99	108
10	10	20	30	40	50	60	70	80	90	100	110	120
11	11	22	33	44	55	66	77	88	99	110	121	132
12	12	24	36	48	60	72	84	96	108	120	132	144

Using What We Know

Exploring Manipulatives

Overview

Students engage in unstructured exploration of manipulatives in preparation for organized use during workstation tasks.

Objectives

- Explore with math manipulatives
- Describe observations using words and pictures.

Procedure

1. Place manipulatives in a workstation and allow students time to explore with them prior to using the manipulative for more formal math activities.

2. Provide drawing or graph paper for students who choose to create drawings of their manipulatives or record their thinking.

3. Consider having students use digital devices to take pictures of their explorations or record one another explaining their observations about the manipulatives.

Differentiation

Because of the nature of this activity, it is accessible to students of all ability levels, and students will naturally differentiate their explorations.

Materials

- manipulatives (e.g., base-ten blocks, linking cubes, pattern blocks)

- digital device (optional)

- drawing or graph paper (optional)

* The *Talking Points* card and these reproducibles are also provided in the Digital Resources (manipulatives.pdf).

Exploring Manipulatives

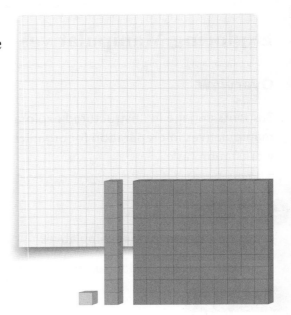

Explore math manipulatives. Describe your observations.

Materials

- math manipulatives
- digital device, drawing paper, or graph paper

Directions

1. Take time to freely explore a math manipulative.

2. Think about how the manipulative might be a useful tool for mathematicians.

3. Record what you observe using words and pictures.

Talking Points

Vocabulary

- manipulative
- attribute
- observe
- observations
- sort

Talk like a mathematician:

An attribute of _____ is _____.

I observe _____.

This manipulative is a useful tool for mathematicians because _____.

This manipulative reminds me of _____.

I can sort my manipulatives by _____.

✂ -

Talking Points

Vocabulary

- manipulative
- attribute
- observe
- observations
- sort

Talk like a mathematician:

An attribute of _____ is _____.

I observe _____.

This manipulative is a useful tool for mathematicians because _____.

This manipulative reminds me of _____.

I can sort my manipulatives by _____.

Using What
We Know

$1,000 House

Overview

Students use base-ten blocks to construct a house "worth" $1,000.

Objective

Generalize place value understanding for multi-digit whole numbers.

Procedure

Note: For this activity, assign base-ten blocks the following values:

- flat = 100

- rod = 10

- unit = 1

1. Distribute copies of the *Building a House* recording sheet (page 45) and other materials to students.

2. Using base-ten blocks, students construct a house with a value of $1,000.

3. Students draw pictorial representations of the materials they used for their houses and the values.

4. Students may use digital devices to photograph their creations.

5. Students may show their thinking in their math journals or on recording sheets.

Differentiation

Change the targeted value of the house to differentiate this activity for **above-level learners** and **below-level learners**.

$1,000 House

Build a house worth
exactly $1,000.

Materials

- base-ten blocks
- digital device (optional)
- *Building a House* recording sheet

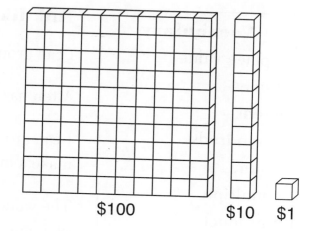

$100 $10 $1

Directions

1. Imagine that each base-ten block has the value shown in the picture.

2. Build a house with a value of exactly $1,000.

3. Take a photo of your house (optional).

4. Explain the value of $1,000 at least two ways.

Talking Points

Vocabulary

- place value
- ones
- tens
- hundreds
- sum
- multiply
- product

Talk like a mathematician:

I can group _____ ones to make a 10.

A ten has the same value as _____ ones.

I can group _____ tens or _____ ones to make a hundred.

The value of a ten is _____ times the value of a one.

The value of a hundred is _____ times the value of a ten.

Talking Points

Vocabulary

- place value
- ones
- tens
- hundreds
- sum
- multiply
- product

Talk like a mathematician:

I can group _____ ones to make a 10.

A ten has the same value as _____ ones.

I can group _____ tens or _____ ones to make a hundred.

The value of a ten is _____ times the value of a one.

The value of a hundred is _____ times the value of a ten.

Name: _____ Date: _____

Building a House

[blank box]

Number used: _____   Value: _____

$100

Number used: _____

Value: _____

$10

Number used: _____

$1

Value: _____

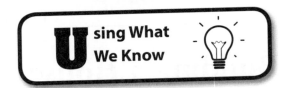

Using What We Know

Choose Sides

Overview

Students decide which of two statements is correct and justify their reasoning using words, numbers, and pictures.

Materials

- *Choose Sides Cards* (pages 49–53)

- *Choose Sides* recording sheet (page 54)

* The *Talking Points* card and these reproducibles are also provided in the Digital Resources (sides.pdf).

Objectives

- Construct viable arguments.

- Critique the reasoning of others.

Procedure

Note: Prior to the lesson, copy the *Choose Sides Cards* (pages 49–53) on cardstock, cut, and laminate. You may choose to have students work in pairs for this activity so they may discuss the problem prior to writing their responses. As a variation on this activity, write problems with multiple-choice answers. Make one mathematician's answer the most commonly wrong answer, and the other mathematician's answer the correct one (e.g., Thomas chose B and Laurie chose D.).

1. Distribute materials to students.

2. Students select a *Choose Sides Card*.

3. After reading and analyzing the problem, students decide which mathematician they agree with.

4. Students justify their reasoning using words, numbers, and pictures.

5. Students may write their answers and explanations in their math journals or on their *Choose Sides* recording sheets (page 54).

Differentiation

- You may choose to have **below-level learners** use recording devices to record their thinking.

- Challenge **above-level learners** to explain not only the statement they agree with but also why the other statement is incorrect.

- Challenge students to create their own *Choose Sides Cards*, which may then be placed in the workstation for other students to solve.

Choose Sides

- -

**Decide which mathematician you agree
with and justify your thinking.**

- -

Materials

- *Choose Sides Cards*
- *Choose Sides* recording sheet

Directions

1. Select a *Choose Sides Card.*

2. Read the statements of both mathematicians.

3. Decide which statement you agree with.

4. Use words, numbers, and pictures to justify your choice.

Becky says that the product of two even factors can be odd. Brandon says the product will always be even. Do you agree with Becky or Brandon? Justify your reasoning with words, numbers, and pictures.

Chris says that the missing factor in the equation $3 \times \square = 15$ is 5. Louis says that it is 12. Do you agree with Chris or Louis? Justify your decision with words, numbers, and pictures.

Talking Points

Vocabulary

- analyze
- justify
- agree
- disagree
- examples
- non-examples
- patterns
- relationships

Talk like a mathematician:

I agree with _____ because _____.

I disagree with _____ because _____.

Would you tell me more about _____?

I notice that _____.

Have you thought about _____?

- -

Talking Points

Vocabulary

- analyze
- justify
- agree
- disagree
- examples
- non-examples
- patterns
- relationships

Talk like a mathematician:

I agree with _____ because _____.

I disagree with _____ because _____.

Would you tell me more about _____?

I notice that _____.

Have you thought about _____?

Choose Sides Cards

Keisha says that $\frac{2}{4}$ is greater than $\frac{3}{6}$. Mark says the fractions are equivalent. Do you agree with Keisha or Mark? Justify your reasoning with words, numbers, and pictures.

Chris says that the missing factor in the equation $3 \times \boxed{} = 15$ is 5. Louis says that it is 12. Do you agree with Chris or Louis? Justify your reasoning with words, numbers, and pictures.

Becky says that the product of two even factors can be odd. Brandon says the product will always be even. Do you agree with Becky or Brandon? Justify your reasoning with words, numbers, and pictures.

Choose Sides Cards *(cont.)*

Jayden says that 647 rounded to the nearest hundred is 600. Emma says it is 650. Do you agree with Jayden or Emma? Justify your reasoning with words, numbers, and pictures.

Gabriel says that $\frac{2}{3}$ and $\frac{4}{6}$ are not equivalent because sixths are smaller pieces than thirds. Mikaila says they are equivalent because they represent the same point on the number line. Do you agree with Gabriel or Mikaila? Justify your reasoning with words, numbers, and pictures.

Shondra says that if she starts watching a 30-minute television show at 11:50 a.m., she will finish watching it at 12:10 p.m. Connor says she will finish watching it at 12:20 p.m. Do you agree with Shondra or Connor? Justify your reasoning with words, numbers, and pictures.

Choose Sides Cards *(cont.)*

Kumar says that a rectangle with a length of 8 cm and a width of 3 cm has a perimeter of 22 cm. William says the perimeter is 11 cm. Do you agree with Kumar or William? Justify your reasoning with words, numbers, and pictures.

Zamari says that a shape can be both a triangle and a quadrilateral. Adrian says that it would have to be one or the other but could not be both. Do you agree with Zamari or Adrian? Justify your reasoning with words, numbers, and pictures.

Louis says that if he partitions a rectangle with an area of 24 cm into four equal parts, each part will have an area of 12 cm. Gwen thinks the area of each part will be 6 cm. Do you agree with Louis or Gwen? Justify your reasoning with words, numbers, and pictures.

Choose Sides Cards *(cont.)*

✂

Parker says that a square with a side length of 6 inches has an area of 36 square inches. Pam says the area would be 24 square inches. Do you agree with Parker or Pam? Justify your reasoning with words, numbers, and pictures.

Iyanna says $\frac{1}{8}$ is greater than $\frac{1}{4}0$, because 8 is greater than 4. Hector says that $\frac{1}{4}$ is greater. Do you agree with Iyanna or Hector? Justify your reasoning with words, numbers, and pictures.

Isaiah says that you cannot have a fraction with the same numerator and denominator, like $\frac{4}{4}$. Brenda says that $\frac{4}{4}$ is equivalent to 1. Do you agree with Isaiah or Brenda? Justify your reasoning with words, numbers, and pictures.

Choose Sides Cards *(cont.)*

Shawna says that to compare $\frac{3}{12}$ and $\frac{2}{4}$ you need to find a common denominator. George says that you do not. Do you agree with Shawna or George? Justify your reasoning with words, numbers, and pictures.

Carlos says that a good estimate of 26×8 is 200. Jeff says his estimate is 240. Do you agree with Carlos or Jeff? Justify your reasoning with words, numbers, and pictures.

Marilyn and Gianna are trying to find the total brownies they will have if Marilyn makes 3 dozen and Gianna makes 4 dozen. Marilyn says the correct equation is $(3 \times 12) + (4 \times 12)$. Gianna says that it is $(3 + 4) \times 12$. Do you agree with Marilyn or Gianna? Justify your reasoning with words, numbers, and pictures.

Name: _____ Date: _____

Choose Sides

_____

_____

_____

_____

_____

_____

Using What We Know

I Wonder...

Overview

Students read stories and write and solve questions that may be answered using information from the story.

Objective

- Make sense of problems.
- Reason about quantities.

Procedure

Note: Prior to the lesson, copy the *I Wonder Cards* (pages 58–60) on cardstock, cut, and laminate. Have students practice reading a story and discuss what they notice about the story (e.g., details, patterns, vocabulary, relationships, connections) in groups prior to using this task in a workstation, and model the process of writing a question for a math problem.

1. Distribute copies of the *What I Wonder* recording sheet (page 61) and other materials to students.

2. For maximum engagement, allow students to choose the story situation they will work with. This task can be used on a rotation basis until students have had a chance to write questions for most or all stories. Students can also write a second, or even third, question for the same story.

3. Have students write wondering questions about the story on their recording sheets or in their math journals. Students then choose one question that can be answered with the information in the story.

4. Students solve the problems in their math journals or on their recording sheets. Encourage students to draw models or pictures to represent their solutions and write equations to describe how they solved them.

5. As a variation, students may exchange questions and solve other students' questions.

Differentiation

- You may choose to scaffold for **below-level learners** by having them start stories with fewer details.

- This task is self-differentiating, as students will write questions at their level of understanding and interest.

Materials

- *I Wonder Cards* (pages 58–60)

- *What I Wonder* recording sheet (page 61)

* The *Talking Points* card and these reproducibles are also provided in the Digital Resources (wonder.pdf).

I Wonder...

Write and solve questions for math stories.

> Somarie made fruit salad for a party. She used 32 ounces of pineapple, 18 ounces of bananas, and some grapes. She used a total of 74 ounces of fruit. After the party, 56 ounces of fruit were left.

Materials

- *I Wonder Cards*
- *What I Wonder* recording sheet

> Christian is raising money for a charity. He saved up $14 from his allowance to donate. His neighbors donated money. Then, he had $30 total. He mowed a lawn for $16 and washed windows for $12.

Directions

1. Select an *I Wonder Card*.

2. Read the story. Pay attention to the details and vocabulary in the story.

3. Write wondering questions about the story on the *What I Wonder* recording sheet or in your math journal. Write questions that can be answered mathematically.

4. From your list, choose the question that interests you the most.

5. Solve your problem in your math journal or on the *What I Wonder* recording sheet. Record your mathematical thinking using precise language, pictures, and numbers.

Talking Points

Vocabulary
• analyze
• justify
• precision
• strategy
• equation

Talk like a mathematician:

I notice _____.

I wonder _____.

I plan to solve this problem by _____.

Drawing a model helps me _____.

The equation _____ could be used to solve this problem.

Talking Points

Vocabulary
• analyze
• justify
• precision
• strategy
• equation

Talk like a mathematician:

I notice _____.

I wonder _____.

I plan to solve this problem by _____.

Drawing a model helps me _____.

The equation _____ could be used to solve this problem.

I Wonder Cards

Somarie made fruit salad for a party. She used 32 ounces of pineapple, 18 ounces of bananas, and some grapes. She used a total of 74 ounces of fruit. After the party, 56 ounces of fruit were left.

Christian is raising money for a charity. He saved up $14 from his allowance to donate. His neighbors donated money. Then, he had $30 total. He mowed a lawn for $16 and washed windows for $12.

Kyoko went to a community baseball game that started at 4:10 p.m. and ended 3 hours and 20 minutes later. It takes 35 minutes to drive from Kyoko's house to the baseball field. Kyoko's dad bought 3 hot dogs and 2 sodas. He spent a total of $13.50 at the game.

I Wonder Cards *(cont.)*

Emily makes quilts for a hobby. Last year, she made 4 quilts and used 28 yards of fabric. She started one quilt on January 14 and finished it on March 2. The fabric she uses usually costs between $8.50 and $13.25 per yard.

Amelia and her dad want to plant a vegetable garden. The length of the garden is 8 feet and the width is 3 feet. Tomato plants need to be planted 1 foot apart. Tomato plants are on sale at Home Warehouse for $2.85 each.

Oscar invited some friends to a backyard campout. There were 16 boys and 3 tents. Oscar's mom bought 2 packages of hot dogs for $3.50 each and 2 packages of buns for $1.85 each. There were 10 hot dogs in each package and 8 buns in each package.

I Wonder Cards *(cont.)*

Colin joined a video game club. The registration fee is $25. Each time he rents a game, it costs $7.50. He can also pay $30 for unlimited rentals in a month. Last month, Colin rented 5 games.

Vinita and Arialye are decorating the gymnasium for a school dance. There are 8 tables. They have 32 balloons and 48 flowers. They expect that 92 students will attend the dance.

Mrs. Lee bought 3 packages of stickers. Each package has 8 sheets of stickers, and each sheet has 24 stickers. On Monday, she gave out 31 stickers, on Tuesday she gave out 28 stickers, and on Wednesday, she gave out 36 stickers.

Name: _____ Date: _____

What I Wonder

Wondering Questions:

1. _____

   _____

2. _____

   _____

3. _____

   _____

Choose one question, and solve it.

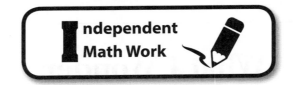

Independent Math Work

You Write the Story

Overview

Students are given equations with unknown numbers. They write story problems represented by the equations, draw mathematical models to show the problems, and solve the equations.

Objective

Represent and solve one- and two-step problems involving all four operations.

Procedure

Note: Prior to the lesson, copy the *You Write the Story Cards* (pages 65–66) on cardstock, cut, and laminate. A blank template is included to create cards for any type of equation: addition, subtraction, multiplication, division, computing with fractions or decimals, algebraic equations, and even multi-step problems.

1. Distribute copies of the *My Story* recording sheet (page 67) and other materials to students.

2. Students choose a card and do the following:

   • Write a story problem based on the equation shown on the card.

   • Draw a math picture or diagram to represent the story problem.

   • Solve for the unknown number in the equation.

3. You may choose to have students show their thinking in their math journals or on their recording sheets.

Differentiation

This activity may be easily differentiated by changing the complexity of the equations that you use.

Materials

• *You Write the Story Cards* (pages 65–66)

• *My Story* recording sheet (page 67)

* The *Talking Points* card and these reproducibles are also provided in the Digital Resources (story.pdf).

You Write the Story

Write a story problem to match an equation.

You Write the Story

422 + 239 = ☐

Materials

- *You Write the Story Cards*
- *My Story* recording sheet

Directions

1. Choose a *You Write the Story Card*.

2. Write a story problem that matches the equation. (Make sure the numbers make sense in your story.)

3. Draw a math picture or diagram to represent the story problem.

4. Solve to find the missing number in the equation.

Talking Points

Vocabulary

- sum
- difference
- addend
- equation
- diagram
- represent

Talk like a mathematician:

I organized my thinking by _____.

The numbers in my story problem are reasonable because _____.

My picture represents my equation because _____.

I can check my solution by _____.

Another way to solve this problem is _____.

✂ -

Talking Points

Vocabulary

- sum
- difference
- addend
- equation
- diagram
- represent

Talk like a mathematician:

I organized my thinking by _____.

The numbers in my story problem are reasonable because _____.

My picture represents my equation because _____.

I can check my solution by _____.

Another way to solve this problem is _____.

You Write the Story Cards

You Write the Story

$$422 + 239 = \boxed{}$$

You Write the Story

$$338 + \boxed{} = 520$$

You Write the Story

$$\boxed{} + 163 = 671$$

You Write the Story

$$735 - 268 = \boxed{}$$

You Write the Story

$$(14 \times 4) - 29 = \boxed{}$$

You Write the Story

$$34 + (6 \times 7) = \boxed{}$$

You Write the Story Cards *(cont.)*

You Write the Story	You Write the Story
You Write the Story	You Write the Story
You Write the Story	You Write the Story

My Story

Directions: Write a story problem that matches your number sentence. Then, draw a math picture or diagram that shows your story problem.

1. _____

_____

_____

_____

2.

3. The missing number is _____.

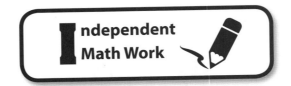

Follow the Rule

- -

Overview

Given an addition or multiplication rule, students will add or multiply numbers in the input column to find the numbers in the output column.

- -

Objective

Generate additive and multiplicative number patterns using an input-output table and given rule.

Procedure

Note: Prior to introducing the workstation task, copy the *Rule Cards* (pages 71–72) and *Input-Output Cards* (pages 73–74) on cardstock, cut, and laminate. Consider copying each set of cards in a different color to make organizing the cards for play easier.

1. Distribute copies of the *Follow the Rule* recording sheet (page 75) and other materials to students.

2. Students place the *Rule Cards* and *Input-Output Cards* facedown in two piles.

3. Students turn over one *Rule Card* and one *Input-Output Card*. They copy the rule in one section of the *Follow the Rule* recording sheet and write the numbers in the input column. There is one additional space for students to add their own input number.

4. Students apply the rule and write the result in the output column.

5. Students repeat with three additional cards.

6. You may choose to collect students' recording sheets or have students glue them in their math journals.

Differentiation

- Provide addition and multiplication charts for **below-level learners**.

- Challenge **above-level learners** to write a formula for the rule using variables *x* and *y*, and graph the pattern on their *Following Rules* graphing sheets (page 76).

- Another option for extending this task is to have students write real-life scenarios for one of the rules.

Materials

- *Rule Cards* (page 71–72)

- *Input-Output Cards* (pages 73–74)

- *Follow the Rule* recording sheet (page 75)

- *Following Rules* graphing sheet (optional) (page 76)

* The *Talking Points* card and these reproducibles are also provided in the Digital Resources (rule.pdf).

Follow the Rule

Generate patterns using an input-output table and a given rule.

Materials

- *Rule Cards*
- *Input-Output Cards*
- *Follow the Rule* recording sheet

Directions

1. Place the *Rule Cards* and *Input-Output* cards facedown in two piles.

2. Turn over one *Rule Card* and one *Input-Output Card*.

3. Write the rule from the *Rule Card* on the *Follow the Rule* recording sheet.

4. Write the input numbers from the *Input-Output Card* in the Input column.

5. Write your own input number in the extra space.

6. Apply the rule to the input numbers to find the output numbers.

7. Repeat with 3 more cards.

Talking Points

Vocabulary

- pattern
- addition pattern
- multiplication pattern
- input-output table
- rule

Talk like a mathematician:

This is an addition pattern because _____.

This is a multiplication pattern because _____.

The relationship between the input and output numbersput numbers is _____.

A pattern I notice in the output numbers is _____.

Talking Points

Vocabulary

- pattern
- addition pattern
- multiplication pattern
- input-output table
- rule

Talk like a mathematician:

This is an addition pattern because _____.

This is a multiplication pattern because _____.

The relationship between the input and output numbersput numbers is _____.

A pattern I notice in the output numbers is _____.

Rule Cards

△ + 10 = □   ▱ + 12 = ⬡

◇ + 6 = ◿   ⏢ + 8 = ◯

□ + 20 = ⬠   ◖ + 7 = ⏢

◯ + 15 = △   ◇ + 100 = ◺

Rule Cards *(cont.)*

⬠ × 2 = ▱

◯ × 4 = ⬡

□ × 5 = ◺

◇ × 7 = ◖

⏢ × 10 = ▭

△ × 100 = ⬡

▱ × 3 = ⬠

▱ × 8 = ⬠

Input-Output Cards

Input	Output
1	
3	
9	
12	

Input	Output
2	
4	
8	
10	

Input	Output
12	
15	
18	
21	

Input	Output
4	
12	
24	
30	

Input-Output Cards *(cont.)*

Input	Output
10	
40	
60	
90	

Input	Output
3	
6	
12	
18	

Input	Output
16	
28	
32	
48	

Input	Output
5	
15	
20	
35	

51729—Guided Math Workstations

Name: _____ Date: _____

Follow the Rule

Rule: _____

Input	Output

Rule: _____

Input	Output

Rule: _____

Input	Output

Rule: _____

Input	Output

Name: _____ Date: _____

Following Rules

Rule: _____

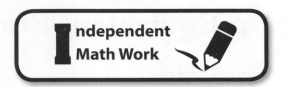

Independent Math Work

Lining Up Equivalent Fractions

Overview

Students identify fractions on number lines, use fraction tiles to create the same fractions, and make equivalent fractions.

Materials

- *Lining Up Equivalent Fractions Cards* (pages 80–83)

- *Line it Up* recording sheet (optional) (page 84)

- fraction tiles

* The *Talking Points* card and these reproducibles are also provided in the Digital Resources (liningup.pdf).

Objective

Demonstrate understanding that a fraction can be shown as a number on a number line and two fractions are equivalent if they are located at the same point on a number line.

Procedure

Note: Prior to the lesson, copy the *Lining Up Equivalent Fractions Cards* (page 80–83) on cardstock. Then, cut and laminate. If fraction tiles aren't available, print and cut copies of *Fraction Tiles* (fractiontiles.pdf) from the Digital Resources.

1. Distribute copies of the *Line it Up* recording sheet (page 84) and other materials to students.

2. Students choose a *Lining Up Equivalent Fractions Card* and identify the fraction shown on the number line.

3. Students use fraction tiles to build the same fraction, relating fractional parts of a whole to the fraction represented on the number line.

4. Students use fraction tiles to find at least one fraction that is equivalent to the fraction on the card.

5. Students sketch all three representations of the fraction: number line representation, matching fraction tiles fraction, and equivalent fraction. Have them repeat with additional cards.

6. You may choose to collect students' recording sheets or have students glue them in their math journals.

Differentiation

- Have **below-level learners** create and name fractions using fraction tiles before moving on to number lines, which are more abstract.

- Challenge **above-level learners** to order the fraction cards from least to greatest.

Lining Up Equivalent Fractions

Represent equivalent fractions multiple ways.

Materials

- *Lining Up Equivalent Fractions Cards*
- fraction tiles
- *Line it Up* recording sheet

Directions

1. Choose a *Lining Up Equivalent Fractions Card*.

2. Sketch the number line. Then, label the fraction represented by the point on your *Line it Up* recording sheet.

3. Use fraction tiles to build the same fraction as the one represented on the number line.

4. Sketch the fraction you created with your fraction tiles on your *Line it Up* recording sheet.

5. Use fraction tiles to build at least one other fraction that is equivalent to the fraction you just built.

6. Sketch the equivalent fraction you created with your fraction tiles on your recording sheet. Remember to label your drawings.

7. Repeat with additional cards.

Talking Points

Vocabulary

- fraction
- numerator
- denominator
- whole
- number line
- equivalent

Talk like a mathematician:

I can identify a fraction on the number line by _____.

In a fraction, the denominator tells _____, and the numerator tells _____.

The fractions _____ and _____ are equivalent because _____.

When fractions are equivalent, I notice _____.

Talking Points

Vocabulary

- fraction
- numerator
- denominator
- whole
- number line
- equivalent

Talk like a mathematician:

I can identify a fraction on the number line by _____.

In a fraction, the denominator tells _____, and the numerator tells _____.

The fractions _____ and _____ are equivalent because _____.

When fractions are equivalent, I notice _____.

Lining Up Equivalent Fractions Cards

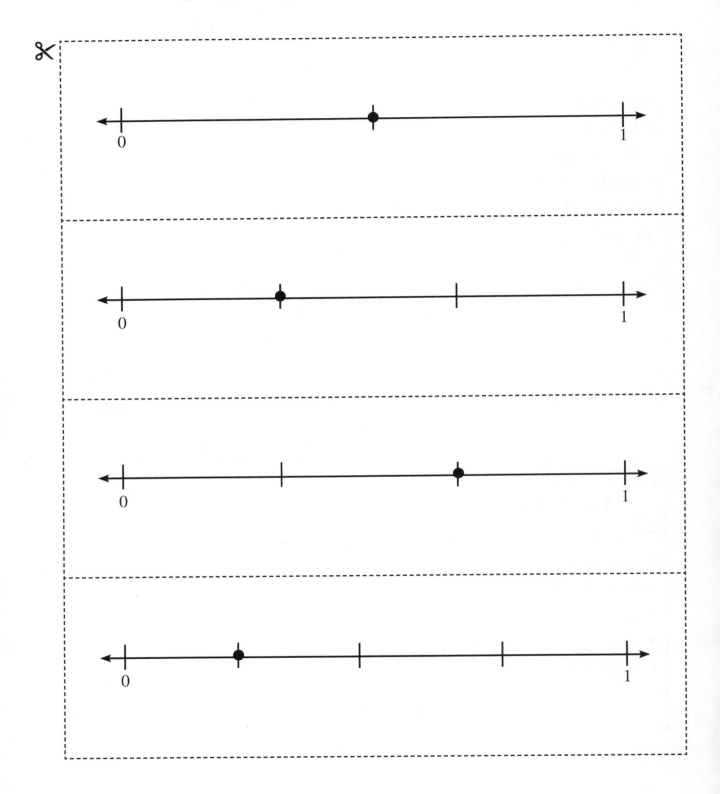

51729—Guided Math Workstations

© *Shell Education*

Lining Up Equivalent Fractions Cards *(cont.)*

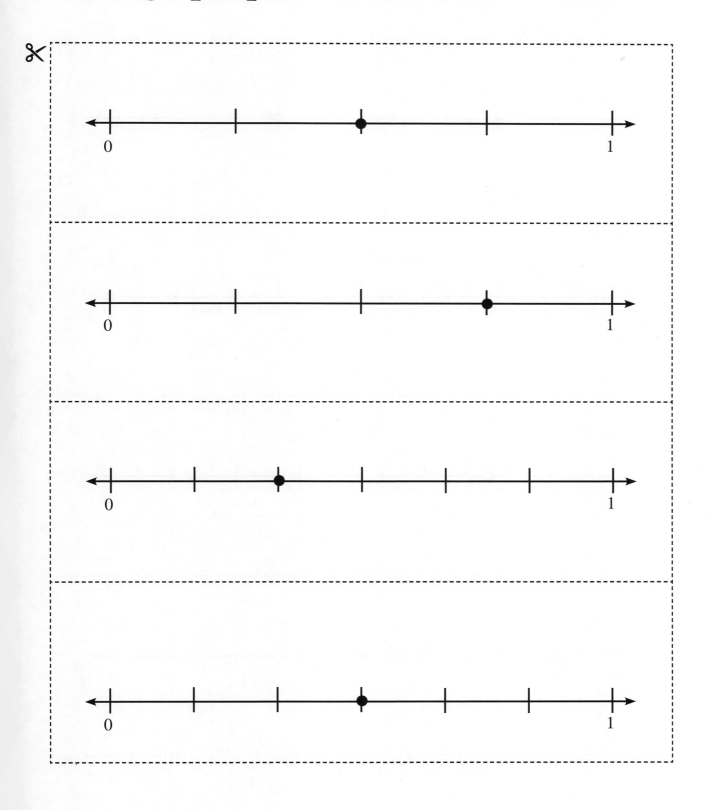

Lining Up Equivalent Fractions Cards *(cont.)*

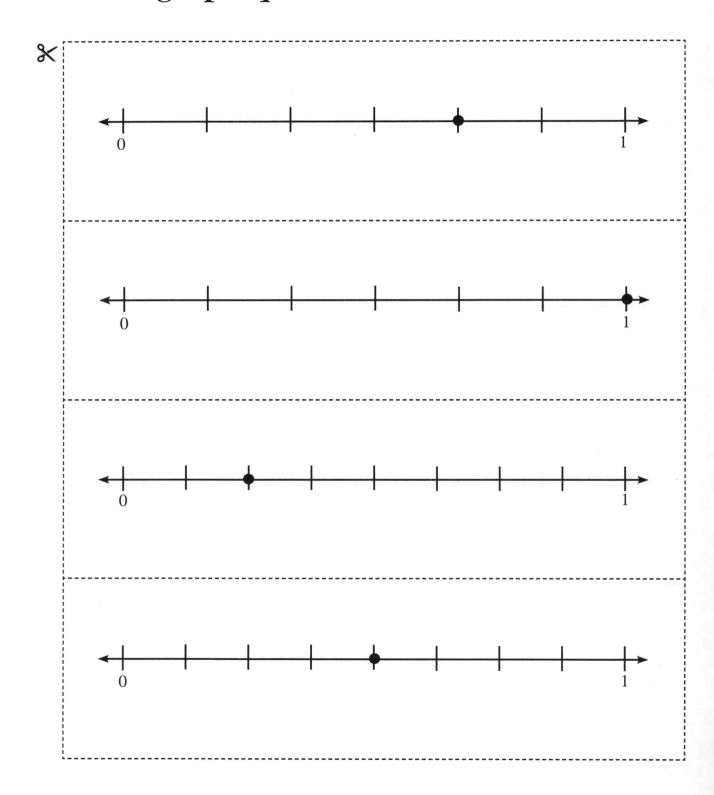

Lining Up Equivalent Fractions Cards *(cont.)*

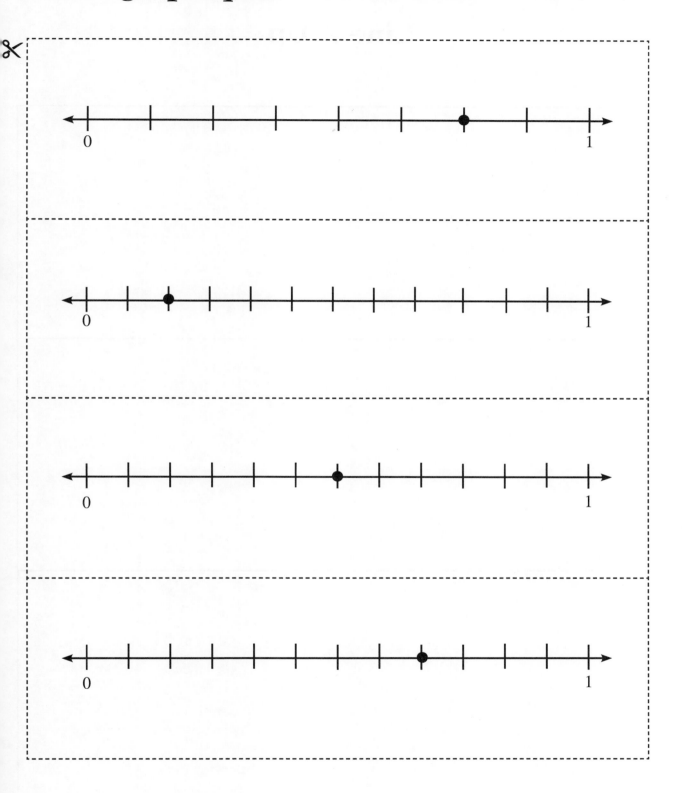

Name: _____ Date: _____

Line it Up

Independent Math Work

Measurement Conversion

- -

Overview

Students solve problems by converting measurements.

- -

Objective

Convert like measurement units within a given measurement system.

Procedure

Note: Prior to the lesson, copy the *Choice Board* (page 88) on cardstock and laminate.

1. Distribute copies of the *Conversion Time* recording sheet (page 89) and other materials to students.

2. Students choose problems that total at least 9 points. The points assigned to each problem indicate the level of difficulty. Two-point problems require only simple conversions. Three- and four-point problems incorporate problem solving. Five-point problems require students to create and solve their own problems. The problems they create may be assigned point values and added to the workstation for other students to solve.

3. You may choose to collect students' recording sheets or have students glue them in their math journals.

Differentiation

- This activity is self-differentiating because students have control over the level of difficulty of the problems they choose to solve.

- Provide conversion charts or pictorial representations of the units for **below-level learners**.

Materials

- *Choice Board* (page 88)

- *Conversion Time* recording sheet (page 89)

* The *Talking Points* card and these reproducibles are also provided in the Digital Resources (conversion.pdf).

Measurement Conversion

Solve problems by converting measurement units within the same measurement system.

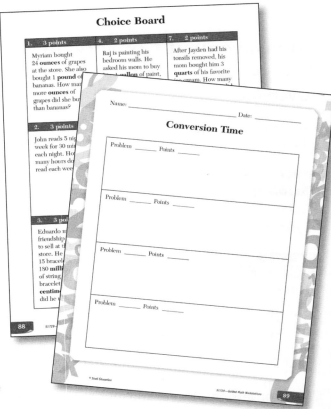

Materials

- *Choice Board*
- *Conversion Time* recording sheet

Directions

1. Choose problems from the *Choice Board* that total at least 9 points. The higher the point value, the more difficult the challenge.

2. Solve the problems on the *Conversion Time* recording sheet. Be sure to explain your thinking using pictures, numbers, and precise mathematical language.

Talking Points

Talk like a mathematician:

The relationship between _____ and _____ is _____.
                            (unit)   (unit)

A pattern I notice when converting from _____ to _____ is _____.
                                         (unit)   (unit)

To convert from _____ to _____, I _____.
                 (unit)   (unit)

Vocabulary

- liquid volume
- mass
- length
- kilometer (km)
- meter (m)
- centimeter (cm)
- kilogram (kg)
- gram (g)

- liter (L)
- milliliter (mL)
- inch (in.)
- foot (ft.)
- yard (yd.)
- mile (mi.)
- ounce (oz.)
- pound (lb.)

- cup (c)
- pint (pt.)
- quart (qt.)
- gallon (gal.)
- hour
- minute
- second

Choice Board

1. 3 points	4. 2 points	7. 2 points
Myriam bought 24 **ounces** of grapes at the store. She also bought 1 **pound** of bananas. How many more **ounces** of grapes did she buy than bananas?	Raj is painting his bedroom walls. He asked his mom to buy him 1 **gallon** of paint, but the paint he wants only comes in **quarts**. How many **quarts** of paint should she buy?	After Jayden had his tonsils removed, his mom bought him 3 **quarts** of his favorite ice cream. How many **pints** of ice cream did Jayden's mom buy?
2. 3 points	**5. 2 points**	**8. 4 points**
John reads 5 nights a week for 30 **minutes** each night. How many **hours** does John read each week?	Todd is training to compete in a 5-**kilometer** race. How many **meters** will he run in the race?	Paula made $2\frac{1}{2}$ **gallons** of lemonade for a birthday party. Alexis made 7 **quarts** of lemonade for the same party. How many **quarts** of lemonade did they make for the party altogether?
3. 3 points	**6. 5 points**	**9. 4 points**
Eduardo made friendship bracelets to sell at the school store. He made 15 bracelets and used 180 **millimeters** of string for each bracelet. How many **centimeters** of string did he use in total?	Write and solve your own problem!	David has a rectangular vegetable garden that is 4 **feet** long and 2 **feet** wide. He makes it larger by adding 1 **foot** to the width. What is the area of the new garden in square **yards**?

51729—Guided Math Workstations

Name: _____ Date: _____

Conversion Time

Problem _____ **Points** _____

Problem _____ **Points** _____

Problem _____ **Points** _____

Problem _____ **Points** _____

Developing Fluency

Numberless Word Problems

Overview

Students choose numbers to use in a word problem, draw a picture and write an equation representing the problem, and solve it.

Objective

- Solve problems with whole numbers using the four operations.

- Represent problems using equations with a letter standing for the unknown quantity.

Procedure

Note: Prior to the lesson, copy and cut apart the *Numberless Word Problems* (pages 93–96).

1. Distribute materials to students. You may choose to select one problem that all students will complete or provide several from which students can select.

2. Students glue their problems into their math journals or on copies of the *Missing Numbers* recording sheet (missingnum.pdf) available in the Digital Resources.

3. Students choose their own numbers to complete the word problems, draw pictures and write equations representing the problems, and solve them. Encourage students to write their answers using complete sentences. (Example: How many pencils did Marla start with? Marla started with _____ pencils.)

Differentiation

- This task is self-differentiating because students will choose numbers they are comfortable working with. Consider providing a range of numbers for students to use to prevent them from using numbers that are either too easy or too challenging.

- Provide manipulatives for **below-level learners** to help them act out the problems.

- Challenge **above-level learners** to represent the problems in more than one way (e.g., picture and number line).

Materials

- *Numberless Word Problems* (pages 93–96)

- *Missing Numbers* recording sheet (missingnum.pdf)

- math journals

- manipulatives (optional)

* The *Talking Points* card and these reproducibles are also provided in the Digital Resources (numberless.pdf).

Numberless Word Problems

Solve problems using the four operations.

Materials

- *Numberless Word Problems*
- math journals
- *Missing Numbers* recording sheet
- manipulatives (optional)

> On a busy Saturday morning, Yummy Bakery sells all _____ doughnuts they made. They sell _____ boxes containing one dozen doughnuts each, and the rest they sell separately.
> How many doughnuts do they sell separately?

> There are _____ puppies and _____ kittens at an animal shelter. During an adoption event, _____ puppies and kittens are adopted.
> How many puppies and kittens are not adopted?

Directions

1. Glue your problem in your math journal or on the *Missing Numbers* recording sheet.

2. Read the word problem. Pay attention to details and vocabulary in the story.

3. Try different numbers in the blanks and act out the problem using manipulatives.

4. Choose numbers that make the most sense. Write them on the blank lines.

5. Draw a picture to show your word problem. Make sure your picture matches the words and numbers in the problem.

6. Write an equation to represent your word problem with a letter standing for the unknown quantity.

7. Solve the problem. Write your answer in a complete sentence. Think about your solution and be sure it makes sense.

Talking Points

Vocabulary
• add
• subtract
• multiply
• divide
• addend
• sum
• difference
• factor
• product
• divisor
• dividend
• quotient

Talk like a mathematician:

When I read the word problem, I noticed _____.

I wondered _____.

This problem reminds me of _____.

My solution makes sense because _____.

Drawing a picture helped me by _____.

My equation represents the problem because _____.

✂ -

Talking Points

Vocabulary
• add
• subtract
• multiply
• divide
• addend
• sum
• difference
• factor
• product
• divisor
• dividend
• quotient

Talk like a mathematician:

When I read the word problem, I noticed _____.

I wondered _____.

This problem reminds me of _____.

My solution makes sense because _____.

Drawing a picture helped me by _____.

My equation represents the problem because _____.

Numberless Word Problems

There are _____ puppies and _____ kittens at an animal shelter. During an adoption event, _____ puppies and kittens are adopted. How many puppies and kittens are not adopted?

Marla has _____ pencils. Stephanie gives her _____ more pencils. Marla shares the pencils equally with her _____ friends and keeps the same amount for herself. How many pencils does Marla give to each of her friends?

There are _____ fewer boys than girls attending Bryant Elementary School. There are _____ boys. How many girls attend Bryant Elementary School? How many students attend Bryant Elementary School altogether?

Numberless Word Problems *(cont.)*

On a busy Saturday morning, Yummy Bakery sells all _____ doughnuts they made. They sell _____ boxes containing one dozen doughnuts each, and the rest they sell separately. How many doughnuts do they sell separately?

The Museum of Natural Science has a large collection containing _____ spiders and _____ insects. Each spider has 8 legs and each insect has 6 legs. How many legs do all the spiders and insects in the collection have?

The school cafeteria has _____ small round tables and _____ large rectangular tables. _____ students can sit at the small tables, and twice as many students can sit at the rectangular tables. How many students can eat in the cafeteria at one time?

Numberless Word Problems *(cont.)*

A football stadium has two large sections and two small sections. Each large section has _____ rows with _____ seats in each row. The two small sections each have _____ rows with _____ seats in each row. How many people does the football stadium hold?

Mrs. Lancaster buys _____ boxes of pencils. Each box contains _____ pencils. During the week, her students use _____ pencils. How many pencils does Mrs. Lancaster have left?

Dion spent _____ minutes cleaning his room and _____ minutes cleaning three other rooms in his house. Each of the other rooms takes _____ minutes to clean. How much time does Dion spend cleaning his house?

Numberless Word Problems *(cont.)*

Roberto earns stickers on rewards charts. He has filled _____ rewards charts with stickers.

Each chart has _____ rows with _____ stickers in each row.

How many stickers has Roberto earned?

REWARD CHART

An office building has a total of _____ offices.

There are _____ offices on each floor.

How many floors does the office building contain?

Jayla has _____ beads for making bracelets.

She will use _____ beads on each bracelet.

How many bracelets can Jayla make?

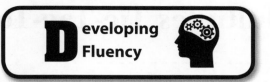

Developing Fluency

Multiples Tic-Tac-Toe

Overview

Students attempt to claim three spaces in a row on the game board by finding multiples of a given factor.

Objective

Determine whether a given whole number is a multiple of a given one-digit number.

Procedure

Note: Prior to introducing the workstation task, make copies of the *Number Cards* (page 100) on cardstock, cut, and laminate. Make copies of the *Multiples Tic-Tac-Toe Game Board* (page 101) on cardstock and laminate them so students can write with dry-erase markers and erase their marks.

1. Distribute materials to students.

2. Players place number cards facedown in a pile, turn over the top card, and write the number in the star labeled "Multiples of…" on the *Multiples Tic-Tac-Toe Game Board*.

3. Players decide who will go first. Then, players take turns claiming spaces by multiplying the factor in the star by the factor in the space and writing the product in the space.

4. The first player to claim three spaces in a row wins.

5. Students may record multiples for each factor in their math journals. Students may also explain patterns they notice in the multiples of the numbers.

Differentiation

- Have **below-level learners** still learning the concept use concrete objects to build each multiple.

- Instruct **above-level learners** to use the *Alternate Number Cards* (page 102) and work with multiples of ten.

Materials

- *Number Cards* (page 100)

- *Multiples Tic-Tac-Toe Game Board* (page 101)

- dry-erase markers in two colors

- *Alternate Numbers Cards* (optional) (page 102)

* The *Talking Points* card and these reproducibles are also provided in the Digital Resources (multiples.pdf).

Multiples Tic-Tac-Toe

Claim three spaces in a row on the game board by finding multiples of a given factor.

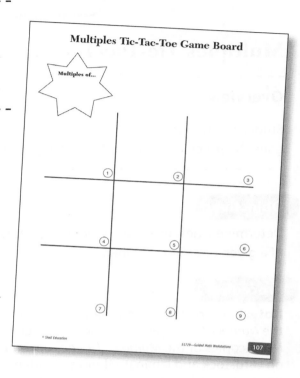

Materials

- *Number Cards*
- *Multiples Tic-Tac-Toe Game Board*
- dry-erase markers in two colors

Directions

1. Shuffle the number cards and place them facedown in a pile.

2. Turn over the top card. Then, write the number in the star labeled "Multiples of…" on the game board.

3. Decide which player will go first.

4. Take turns claiming spaces on the *Multiples Tic-Tac-Toe Game Board* by multiplying the factor in the star by the factor shown in a space. Write the product of the two factors in the same space.

5. Mark three spaces in a row to win!

Talking Points

Vocabulary
- factor
- product
- multiply
- multiple

Talk like a mathematician:

_____ is the product of _____ and _____.

_____ is a multiple of _____.

The strategy I used is _____.

Factors and multiples are related because _____.

A pattern I notice in the multiples of _____ is _____.

Talking Points

Vocabulary
- factor
- product
- multiply
- multiple

Talk like a mathematician:

_____ is the product of _____ and _____.

_____ is a multiple of _____.

The strategy I used is _____.

Factors and multiples are related because _____.

A pattern I notice in the multiples of _____ is _____.

Number Cards

2	3	4
5	6	7
8	9	10
11	12	

Multiples Tic-Tac-Toe Game Board

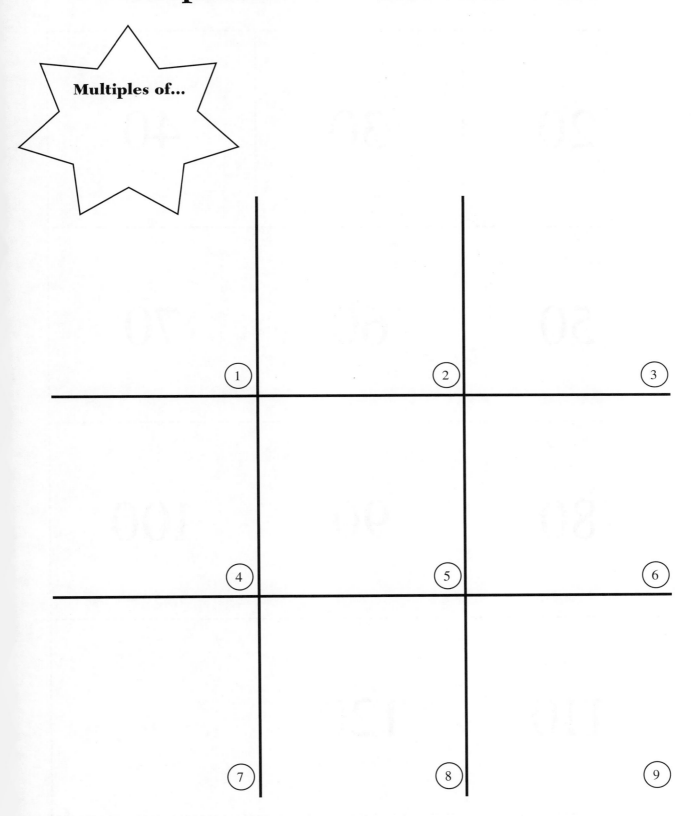

Multiples of...

①   ②   ③

④   ⑤   ⑥

⑦   ⑧   ⑨

Alternate Number Cards

20	30	40
50	60	70
80	90	100
110	120	

51729—Guided Math Workstations

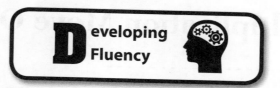

Developing Fluency

Multiplication Move One

Overview

Students change one factor to capture a space on the game board. The first player to get four in a row wins.

Objective

Multiply factors to build automaticity with math facts.

Procedure

Note: Prior to the lesson, copy *Multiplication Move One Game Board* (page 106) on cardstock and laminate or place in a sheet protector.

1. Distribute materials to students.

2. Player 1 places paper clips on two factors, multiplies to find the product, and marks a space with the product on the game board.

3. Player 2 moves only one paper clip to a different factor, multiplies, and marks a space with the product on the game board. Both paper clips may be placed on the same factor.

4. Players use *X*s and *O*s or different colored markers to differentiate their marks.

5. The first player to claim four spaces in a row wins.

6. Students may record facts from each of their turns in their math journals. Students may also record videos explaining their strategies and reflecting on changes they might make when playing the game again.

Differentiation

- Distribute copies of the *Multiplication/Division Chart* (page 107) or manipulatives to students who need concrete support.

- Create a game board with fewer products to focus on specific facts for **below-level learners**. For example, make a game board with only the products for the factors 0–5 to develop automaticity with those facts.

Materials

- *Multiplication Move One Game Board* (page 106)

- 2 paper clips

- dry-erase markers

- *Multiplication/Division Chart* (optional) (page 107)

* The *Talking Points* card and these reproducibles are also provided in the Digital Resources (moveone.pdf).

Multiplication Move One

Choose factors to capture four spaces in a row on the game board.

Materials

- *Multiplication Move One Game Board*
- 2 paper clips
- dry-erase markers

Directions

1. Choose which player will go first.

2. Take turns:

   - Place paper clips on two factors.
   - Multiply to find the product.
   - Mark a space with that product on the game board. Both paper clips may be placed on the same factor (e.g., 3 and 3).
   - Move one paper clip to a different factor, multiply to find the product, and mark a space with that product on the game board.

3. Mark 4 spaces in a row to win!

Multiplication Move One Game Board

64	20	8	54	18	28	8	27
12	40	24	81	20	25	14	35
48	16	6	30	10	42	63	24
10	49	20	15	32	21	12	63
56	28	42	14	72	18	45	54
16	6	36	12	49	32	10	40
72	21	16	81	8	64	21	45
14	25	30	24	48	6	35	18

2 3 4 5 6 7 8 9

Talking Points

Vocabulary
- factor
- product
- multiply

Talk like a mathematician:

I marked _____ because _____ multiplied by _____ equals _____.

_____ is the product of _____ and _____.

I chose the factors _____ and _____ because they have a product of _____.

____ × ____ = ____ is related to ____ ÷ ____ = ____.

The strategy I used to pick my factors is _____.

Talking Points

Vocabulary
- factor
- product
- multiply

Talk like a mathematician:

I marked _____ because _____ multiplied by _____ equals _____.

_____ is the product of _____ and _____.

I chose the factors _____ and _____ because they have a product of _____.

____ × ____ = ____ is related to ____ ÷ ____ = ____.

The strategy I used to pick my factors is _____.

Multiplication Move One Game Board

64	20	8	54	18	28	8	27
12	40	24	81	20	25	14	35
48	16	6	30	10	42	63	24
10	49	20	15	32	21	12	63
56	28	42	14	72	18	45	54
16	6	36	12	49	32	10	40
72	21	16	81	8	64	21	45
14	25	30	24	48	6	35	18

2 3 4 5 6 7 8 9

Multiplication/Division Chart

×/÷	1	2	3	4	5	6	7	8	9
1	1	2	3	4	5	6	7	8	9
2	2	4	6	8	10	12	14	16	18
3	3	6	9	12	15	18	21	24	27
4	4	8	12	16	20	24	28	32	36
5	5	10	15	20	25	30	35	40	45
6	6	12	18	24	30	36	42	48	54
7	7	14	21	28	35	42	49	56	63
8	8	16	24	32	40	48	56	64	72
9	9	18	27	36	45	54	63	72	81

Developing
Fluency

Twenty-One

Overview

Students combine four numbers, using any operation, to create an expression that produces the smallest difference from 21.

Objective

Use whole number operations to interpret numerical expressions.

Procedure

1. Distribute copies of the *Twenty One* recording sheet (page 111) and other materials to students.

2. Players roll a number cube four times and record the digits on their *Twenty-One* recording sheets.

3. Players use the numbers rolled and any combination of operations to create and evaluate expressions.

4. The player with the smallest difference from 21 earns 1 point. If both players have the same difference, each player scores 1 point. Any player scoring 21 exactly scores 2 points.

5. The player with the most points after five rounds wins.

6. You may choose to collect students' recording sheets or have students glue them in their math journals. Or, students may post their most creative expressions on a Twenty-One poster or wall display.

Differentiation

- Have **below-level learners** start by rolling only three numbers instead of four.

- You may choose to have **below-level learners** reference copies of the *Multiplication/Division Chart* (page 112) for additional support.

- Challenge **above-level learners** to use five numbers or use exponents.

Materials

- number cube

- *Twenty-One* recording sheet (page 111)

- *Multiplication/Division Chart* (optional) (page 112)

* The *Talking Points* card and these reproducibles are also provided in the Digital Resources (twentyone.pdf).

Twenty-One

Create an expression with four numbers that produces the smallest difference from 21.

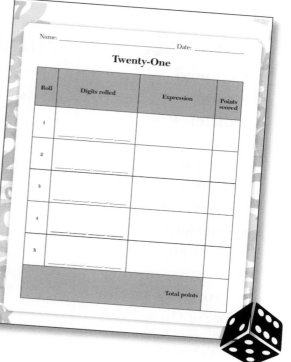

Materials

- number cube
- *Twenty-One* recording sheet

Directions

1. Roll the number cube four times.

2. Record the numbers rolled on the *Twenty-One* recording sheet.

3. Create an expression by using the numbers rolled and any combination of operations (addition, subtraction, multiplication, or division). Remember to use parentheses correctly and evaluate your expression following the order of operations.

4. The player with the smallest difference from 21 earns 1 point. If there is a tie, each player scores 1 point. Earn 2 points for getting 21 exactly.

5. The player who earns the most points after 5 rounds wins!

Talking Points

Vocabulary	Talk like a mathematician:
• addend • sum • difference • factor • product • divisor • dividend • quotient • evaluate • expression • grouping symbol • parentheses	The order in which I perform operations is important because _____. Grouping symbols are important because _____. The difference between my number and 21 is _____. The first thing I did to evaluate my expression was _____ because _____.

✂ ┈┈

Talking Points

Vocabulary	Talk like a mathematician:
• addend • sum • difference • factor • product • divisor • dividend • quotient • evaluate • expression • grouping symbol • parentheses	The order in which I perform operations is important because _____. Grouping symbols are important because _____. The difference between my number and 21 is _____. The first thing I did to evaluate my expression was _____ because _____.

Name: _____ Date: _____

Twenty-One

Roll	Digits rolled	Expression	Points scored
1	_____ , _____ , _____ , _____		
2	_____ , _____ , _____ , _____		
3	_____ , _____ , _____ , _____		
4	_____ , _____ , _____ , _____		
5	_____ , _____ , _____ , _____		
		Total points	

Multiplication/Division Chart

×/÷	1	2	3	4	5	6	7	8	9
1	1	2	3	4	5	6	7	8	9
2	2	4	6	8	10	12	14	16	18
3	3	6	9	12	15	18	21	24	27
4	4	8	12	16	20	24	28	32	36
5	5	10	15	20	25	30	35	40	45
6	6	12	18	24	30	36	42	48	54
7	7	14	21	28	35	42	49	56	63
8	8	16	24	32	40	48	56	64	72
9	9	18	27	36	45	54	63	72	81

Developing
Fluency

Par for the Course

Overview

Players add, subtract, and multiply numbers rolled on number cubes to compete on an 18-hole golf course. The player with the fewest strokes wins the game.

Materials

• 2 number cubes

• *Par for the Course* recording sheet (page 116)

• *Multiplication/Division Chart* (optional) (page 117)

• *Addition/Subtraction Chart* (optional) (page 118)

* The *Talking Points* card and these reproducibles are also provided in the Digital Resources (par.pdf).

Objective

Add, subtract, and multiply to build automaticity with math facts.

Procedure

1. Distribute copies of the *Par for the Course* recording sheet (page 116) and other materials to students.

2. Each "hole" has a different objective. Player 1 rolls two number cubes as many times as necessary to meet the goal of the hole. For example, on Hole 3, students must roll a sum less than 6. Each time students roll, it counts as a stroke. A player must keep rolling until he or she meets the goal of that hole.

3. When the goal is met, Player 1 records his or her score and proof of score on the recording sheet. The score is the number of times the number cubes were rolled.

4. Player 2 repeats the process for Hole 1.

5. Play continues until all 18 holes have been played. The player with the lowest total score wins.

6. You many choose to collect students' recording sheets.

Differentiation

• You may choose to provide **below-level learners** with concrete objects to represent each roll as a tracking strategy. Provide copies of the *Multiplication/Division Chart* (page 117) or *Addition/Subtraction Chart* (page 118) to students who still need concrete support.

• Challenge **above-level learners** to work with larger numbers by using a 10-sided die (0–9).

• Challenge **above-level learners** to determine what par should be for each hole, based on the probability of rolling numbers that meet the objective.

(Adapted from MathNook 2016)

Par for the Course

Meet the goal for each hole on this golf course with the fewest strokes possible.

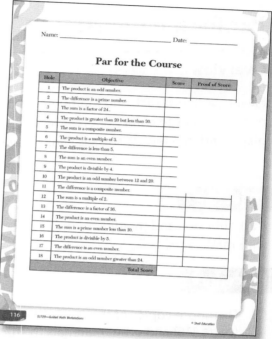

Materials

- 2 number cubes
- *Par for the Course* recording sheet

Directions

1. Take turns:

   - Roll the number cubes until you meet the goal. Each roll counts as one stroke. For example, if it takes you 7 rolls to meet the goal, your score is 7.
   - When your roll meets the goal, record the equation in the Proof of Score column. Write how many strokes it took to meet the goal in the Score column.

2. Complete all 18 holes, and add your total strokes. Earn the lowest score to win!

Talking Points

Vocabulary
- sum
- addend
- difference
- product
- factor
- odd
- even
- multiple
- greater than
- less than
- divisible
- prime
- composite

Talk like a mathematician:

_____ is odd because _____.

_____ is even because _____.

_____ is composite because _____.

_____ is prime because _____.

The product of my factors is _____.

The sum of my addends is _____.

The difference of my numbers is _____.

I know _____ is divisible by _____ because _____.

Talking Points

Vocabulary
- sum
- addend
- difference
- product
- factor
- odd
- even
- multiple
- greater than
- less than
- divisible
- prime
- composite

Talk like a mathematician:

_____ is odd because _____.

_____ is even because _____.

_____ is composite because _____.

_____ is prime because _____.

The product of my factors is _____.

The sum of my addends is _____.

The difference of my numbers is _____.

I know _____ is divisible by _____ because _____.

Par for the Course

Hole	Objective	Score	Proof of Score
1	The product is an odd number.		
2	The difference is a prime number.		
3	The sum is a factor of 24..		
4	The product is greater than 20 but less than 30.		
5	The sum is a composite number.		
6	The product is a multiple of 3.		
7	The difference is less than 5.		
8	The sum is an even number.		
9	The product is divisible by 4.		
10	The product is an odd number between 12 and 20.		
11	The difference is a composite number.		
12	The sum is a multiple of 2.		
13	The difference is a factor of 36.		
14	The product is an even number.		
15	The sum is a prime number less than 10.		
16	The product is divisible by 5.		
17	The difference is an even number.		
18	The product is an odd number greater than 24.		
	Total Score		

Multiplication/Division Chart

×/÷	1	2	3	4	5	6	7	8	9
1	1	2	3	4	5	6	7	8	9
2	2	4	6	8	10	12	14	16	18
3	3	6	9	12	15	18	21	24	27
4	4	8	12	16	20	24	28	32	36
5	5	10	15	20	25	30	35	40	45
6	6	12	18	24	30	36	42	48	54
7	7	14	21	28	35	42	49	56	63
8	8	16	24	32	40	48	56	64	72
9	9	18	27	36	45	54	63	72	81

Addition/Subtraction Chart

+/−	1	2	3	4	5	6	7	8	9	10
1	2	3	4	5	6	7	8	9	10	11
2	3	4	5	6	7	8	9	10	11	12
3	4	5	6	7	8	9	10	11	12	13
4	5	6	7	8	9	10	11	12	13	14
5	6	7	8	9	10	11	12	13	14	15
6	7	8	9	10	11	12	13	14	15	16
7	8	9	10	11	12	13	14	15	16	17
8	9	10	11	12	13	14	15	16	17	18
9	10	11	12	13	14	15	16	17	18	19
10	11	12	13	14	15	16	17	18	19	20

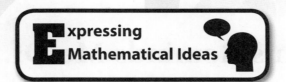

Expressing **Mathematical Ideas**

This Reminds Me Of…

Overview

Students analyze a picture of a model and make mathematical connections by looking for details, patterns, and relationships.

Materials

- *This Reminds Me Of…* (page 122)

- *Mathematical Models* (pages 123–124)

- glue or tape

- student photographs (optional)

* The *Talking Points* card and these reproducibles are also provided in the Digital Resources (remindsme.pdf).

Objective

Recognize connections between mathematical concepts and use precise language to communicate relationships.

Procedure

Note: Prior to introducing the workstation task, copy and cut the *Mathematical Models* (pages 123–124) into strips. Look through other teaching resources to find additional mathematical models.

1. Distribute copies of the *This Reminds Me Of…* recording sheet (page 122) and other materials to students.

2. Students choose a strip with a picture of a model, glue or tape it into the space just below "This reminds me of…" on the recording sheet, and describe their connections. For example, a number line with markings between the whole numbers should connect to fractions or decimals. A picture showing equal groups should trigger a connection to multiplication or division. Likewise, students might make connections between pictures of base-ten blocks and place value.

3. Create a display using photographs and students' recording sheets.

4. You may choose to collect students' recording sheets or have students glue them in their math journals.

Differentiation

- For **below-level learners**, provide a choice of several concepts that may be related to the picture and let them choose one. For example, you might give students a card with the words *addition*, *multiplication*, and *fractions* to accompany a model. They may choose the word they think has a connection to the model and then write an explanation.

- Have **above-level learners** write a story problem related to the model.

This Reminds Me Of...

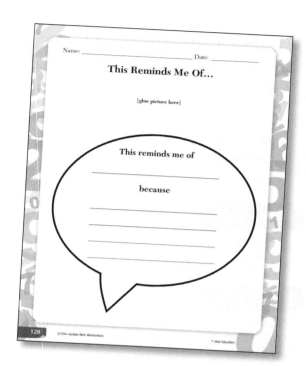

**Analyze a model and make
mathematical connections.**

Materials

- *Mathematical Models*
- glue or tape
- *This Reminds Me Of...* recording sheet

Directions

1. Choose a mathematical model and glue or
   tape it on your recording sheet in the space labeled "glue picture here."

2. Carefully observe your model like a mathematician, looking for details,
   patterns, and relationships. What do you notice? What does it remind
   you of? Be sure to spend enough time on this step.

3. Complete your recording sheet as follows:

   - **This reminds me of**—What mathematical concept does this picture make
     you think of?
   - **Because**—What is it about the picture that creates that connection?

4. Remember to use precise mathematical language.

Talking Points

Vocabulary

- connection
- notice
- observe
- pattern
- diagram
- model
- justify

Talk like a mathematician:

This model reminds me of _____ because _____.

I noticed _____.

_____ and _____ are related because _____.

I made a connection between _____ and _____ because _____.

Talking Points

Vocabulary

- connection
- notice
- observe
- pattern
- diagram
- model
- justify

Talk like a mathematician:

This model reminds me of _____ because _____.

I noticed _____.

_____ and _____ are related because _____.

I made a connection between _____ and _____ because _____.

Name: _____ Date: _____

This Reminds Me Of...

[glue picture here]

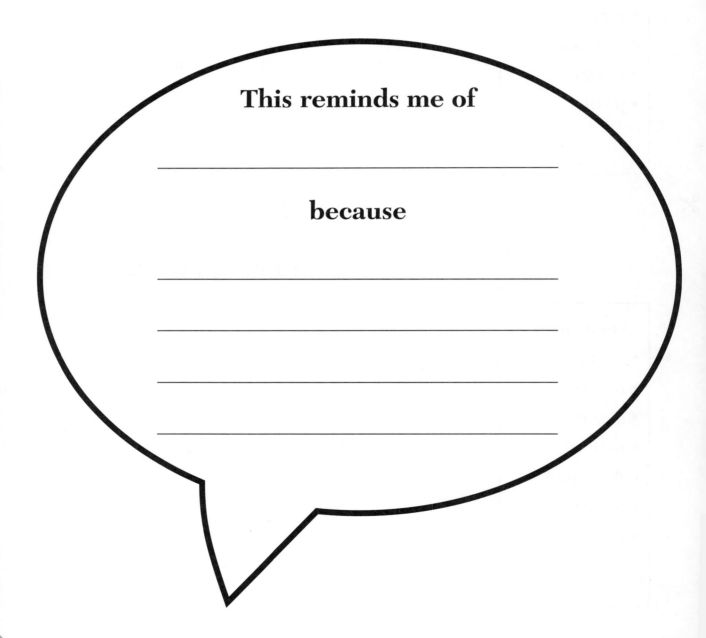

This reminds me of

_____

because

_____

_____

_____

_____

Mathematical Models

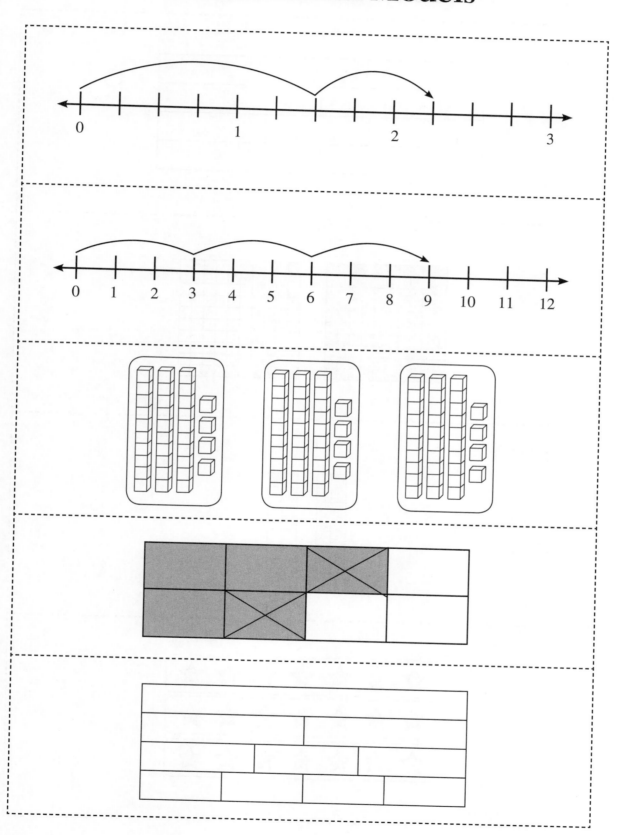

Mathematical Models *(cont.)*

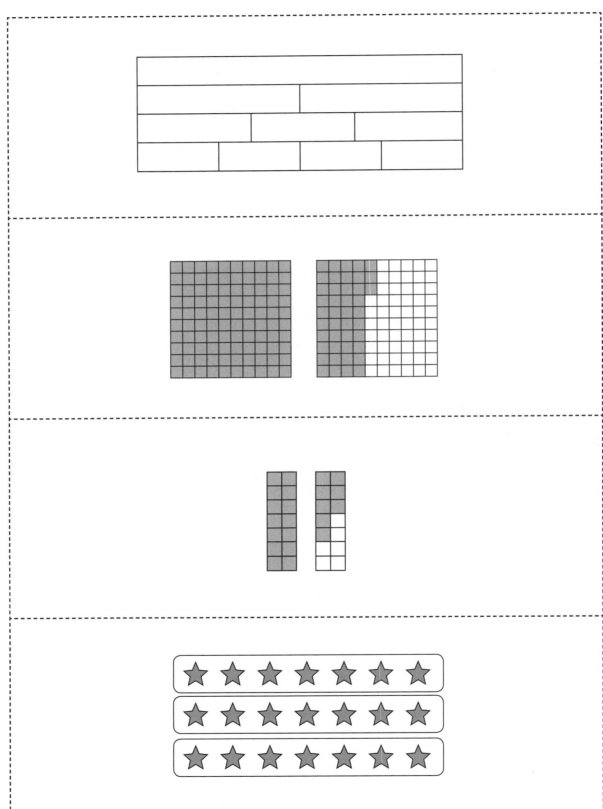

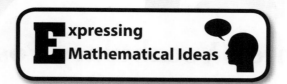

Wanted Vocabulary Poster

- -

Overview

Students create a wanted poster for a vocabulary term using words and pictures.

- -

Objective

Use precise language to communicate mathematical ideas and make connections between related mathematical concepts.

Procedure

1. Distribute copies of the *Wanted Poster* (page 128) and other materials to students. You might assign the words or let students choose.

2. Students complete the *Wanted Poster* as follows:

   - **Name**: vocabulary term

   - **Description**: definition of term in students' own words

   - **Picture**: drawing showing vocabulary term

   - **Known Associates**: other vocabulary terms related to word

3. You may choose to collect and display students' posters.

Differentiation

- Support **below-level learners** by assigning them a vocabulary word that will help develop deeper understandings of a concept.

- Challenge **above-level learners** to use the copies of the *Dangerous Duo* (page 129) to compare two vocabulary terms.

Materials

- *Wanted Poster* (page 128)

- colored pencils

- Math Word Wall or list of vocabulary terms

- *Dangerous Duo* (page 129)

* The *Talking Points* card and these reproducibles are also provided in the Digital Resources (poster.pdf).

Wanted Vocabulary Poster

Create a wanted poster describing a math vocabulary term using words and pictures.

Materials

- *Wanted Poster*
- crayons or colored pencils

Directions

1. Think deeply about everything you know about your vocabulary word.

2. Complete your poster as follows:

   - **Name**: Write down your vocabulary term.
   - **Description**: What does this term mean in your own words?
   - **Picture**: How can you illustrate this word?
   - **Known Associates**: What other math ideas are connected to this word?

3. Remember to use precise mathematical language.

Talking Points

Vocabulary
• model
• diagram
• pictorial representation
• connection
• precise

Talk like a mathematician:

An example of _____ is _____ because _____.

My picture shows _____.

The most important thing about _____ is _____.

_____ relates to _____ because _____.

A non-example of _____ is _____ because _____.

I made a connection between _____ and _____ because _____.

✂ -

Talking Points

Vocabulary
• model
• diagram
• pictorial representation
• connection
• precise

Talk like a mathematician:

An example of _____ is _____ because _____.

My picture shows _____.

The most important thing about _____ is _____.

_____ relates to _____ because _____.

A non-example of _____ is _____ because _____.

I made a connection between _____ and _____ because _____.

Name: _____ Date: _____

WANTED

Name: _____

Description

_____

_____

_____

_____

_____

Picture

Known Associates

Name: _____ Date: _____

DANGEROUS DUO

Picture	Picture

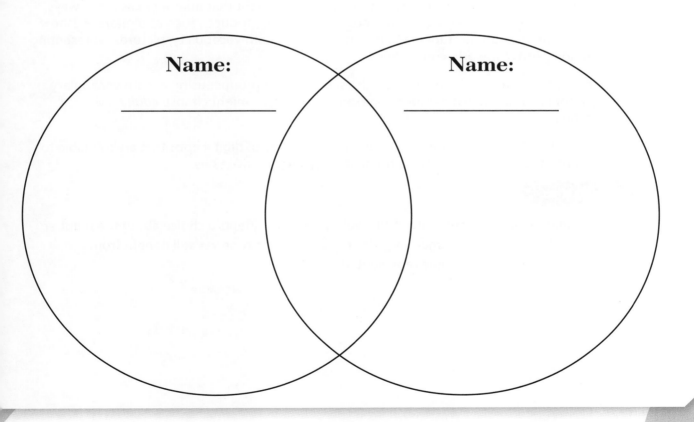

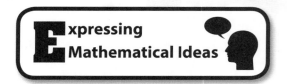

Expressing Mathematical Ideas

All About...

Overview

Students create a poster or digital presentation about a specific number or math topic.

Materials

- chart paper

- colored pencils or markers

- devices for taking photographs or videos and for creating a digital presentation (optional)

* The *Talking Points* card and these reproducibles are also provided in the Digital Resources (allabout.pdf).

Objective

Use precise mathematical language, numbers, and/or drawings to represent a mathematical concept.

Procedure

Note: This activity is purposefully unstructured to allow for a great deal of student choice and creativity. You may structure it as an activity to be completed in one class period or allow students to stretch it into a longer project.

1. Distribute materials to students.

2. One option is for students to choose a number and represent that number in as many ways as possible. Have students create either posters or digital products, such as digital slideshow presentations. Encourage students to include relevant math vocabulary, pictures representing the number, and real-world connections.

3. Another option is for students to create the same type of product using a math vocabulary term or topic, rather than a number. For example, students might choose *addition* or *subtraction*.

4. This type of activity allows students to use a wide variety of digital apps that are available to create a product, rather than just using digital apps to practice skills.

Differentiation

This activity adjusts easily for students of all levels. Offering students a choice about the number or topic allows them to choose something within their comfort zone yet still benefit from expressing their ideas using multiple representations.

All About...

Create a product to communicate everything you know about a number or a math vocabulary term.

Materials

- chart paper
- crayons, colored pencils, or markers
- devices for taking photographs or videos and for creating a digital presentation (optional)

Directions

1. Choose a number, vocabulary word, or math topic.

2. Use words, numbers, and pictures to show everything you can about your number, word, or topic.

3. If you choose a number, think about:

   - different ways to represent the number
   - examples in everyday life
   - personal connections
   - related vocabulary

4. If you choose a vocabulary word or math topic, think about:

   - the meaning of the word
   - pictures or drawings that show the meaning
   - examples and non-examples
   - connections to everyday life
   - related math ideas

Talking Points

Vocabulary

- connections
- diagram
- goal
- justify
- model
- observe
- represent

Talk like a mathematician:

I made a connection between _____ and _____ because _____.

I can represent this number in multiple ways by _____.

This word reminds me of _____.

Clearly communicating my ideas is important because _____.

Talking Points

Vocabulary

- connections
- diagram
- goal
- justify
- model
- observe
- represent

Talk like a mathematician:

I made a connection between _____ and _____ because _____.

I can represent this number in multiple ways by _____.

This word reminds me of _____.

Clearly communicating my ideas is important because _____.

References Cited

Diller, Debbie. 2011. *Math Work Stations: Independent Learning You Can Count On, K–2*. Portland: Stenhouse Publishers.

Mathnook. 2016. "MathPup Golf." Cool Math Games for Kids. Last modified November 29, 2016. www.mathnook.com

Sammons, Laney. 2010. *Guided Math: A Framework for Mathematics Instruction*. Huntington Beach: Shell Education.

———. 2013. *Strategies for Implementing Guided Math*. Huntington Beach: Shell Education.

———. 2014. *Guided Math Conferences*. Huntington Beach: Shell Education.

Answer Key

Choice Board (page 88)

1. 8 more oz. of grapes

2. 2.5 hours

3. 270 centimeters

4. 4 quarts

5. 5,000 meters

6. Answers will vary.

7. 6 pints

8. 17 quarts

9. 4 yards

Digital Resources

Page(s)	Resource	Filename
16–22	Area and Perimeter War	war.pdf
24–28	Difference from 5,000	difference.pdf
30–32	On a Roll	roll.pdf
34–38	Equivalent Fractions	equivalent.pdf
40–41	Exploring Manipulatives	manipulatives.pdf
43–45	$1,000 House	house.pdf
47–54	Choose Sides	sides.pdf
56–61	I Wonder…	wonder.pdf
63–67	You Write the Story	story.pdf
69–76	Follow the Rule	rule.pdf
78–84	Lining Up Equivalent Fractions	liningup.pdf
86–89	Measurement Conversion	conversions.pdf
91–96	Numberless Word Problems	numberless.pdf
98–102	Multiples Tic-Tac-Toe	multiples.pdf
104–107	Multiplication Move One	moveone.pdf
109–112	Twenty-One	twentyone.pdf
114–118	Par for the Course	par.pdf
120–124	This Reminds Me Of…	remindsme.pdf
126–129	Wanted Vocabulary Poster	poster.pdf
131–132	All About…	allabout.pdf
—	*Fraction Tiles*	fractiontiles.pdf
—	*Missing Numbers* recording sheet	missingnum.pdf

Notes

Notes